Japan
Style
Sheet

Japan Style Sheet

The SWET Guide
for Writers, Editors and Translators

REVISED EDITION

Society of Writers, Editors and Translators
Tokyo, Japan

Stone Bridge Press • Berkeley, California

Published by

Stone Bridge Press, P. O. Box 8208, Berkeley, CA 94707

TEL 510-524-8732 • FAX 510-524-8711 • E-MAIL sbp@stonebridge.com

For correspondence, updates, and further information about this
and other Stone Bridge Press books, visit Stone Bridge Press
online at www.stonebridge.com.

Cover calligraphy and design by Linda Thurston

Originally published as *Japan Style Sheet* in Tokyo, Japan, 1983

Revised edition, 1998

© 1983, 1998 Society of Writers, Editors and Translators, Tokyo, Japan

LIBRARY OF CONGRESS CATALOGING-IN-PUBLICATION DATA

Japan style sheet: the SWET guide for writers, editors, and translators.—Rev. ed.
     p.   cm.
    Includes bibliographical references and index.
    ISBN-13: 978-1-880656-30-3
    ISBN-10: 1-880656-30-2
    1. Japanese language—Style—Handbooks, manuals, etc.
2. Authorship—Style manuals—Handbooks, manuals, etc. 3. English
language—Style—Handbooks, manuals, etc. 4. Japan—Handbooks, manuals, etc.
I. Society of Writers, Editors and Translators (Japan)
PL635.J36   1998
808'.027—dc21   98-12587
                                                     CIP

Contents

Preface to the Revised Edition

This guide has been compiled to assist writers, editors, and translators working on English-language publications related to Japan. It discusses problems that come up in connection with Japanese names and dates, and, most important, with the use of the Japanese language transcribed into the Latin alphabet. While it contains advice, information, and several appendices useful to translators and researchers in Japanese studies, it is mainly aimed at the needs of editors and writers without specialized knowledge of Japan or the Japanese language.

Topics discussed in this book include romanization systems and methods of indicating long vowels, apostrophes, and other aids to a proper reading of romanized Japanese words; spelling; use of hyphens; italicization; personal names and place names; capitalization; plurals; and styles for notes and other backmatter.

The first edition of *Japan Style Sheet* was compiled in 1983 on the basis of the editorial styles of major publications and publishers whose work focused on Japan. Through quoting the preferred styles of respected journals and editorial offices, we presented options for solving the most common text-handling problems.

This new edition has been revised to respond to (1) the disappearance from the publishing scene of several of the authorities quoted in the first edition; (2) the call for a guide that presents alternative styles clearly and succinctly and prescribes particular styles for specific types of publications; and (3) the needs of a wider variety of editors, journalists, and writers dealing with Japan.

In the fifteen years since the first edition of *Japan Style Sheet*

ABOUT THE SIDEBARS

Throughout this book are sidebars that contain additional commentary about subjects that are discussed in the main text or that are not strictly about stylistic concerns.

FOR GENERAL STYLE QUESTIONS

Many of the problems writers and editors of Japan-related material need to solve are no different from those occasioned by non-Japan-related texts. *The Chicago Manual of Style* is an excellent guide to nearly every aspect of word handling in publications and should be consulted for general questions not addressed in this book. *The Chicago Manual* includes some reliable material on handling Japanese, but may be more useful for its discussions of Chinese and other languages frequently encountered by editors of Japan- or Asia-related publications.

was published, writing about Japan has greatly proliferated. Professionals responsible for Japan-related material—books, magazines, newspaper columns, technical manuals, advertising, government documents, art exhibition catalogs—are more numerous and diverse. The readers of some of these publications can be expected to know something about Japan and the Japanese language; audiences for other works may not have such knowledge. The style decisions that editors make should be based on the audience they intend to reach. The information in this guide is intended to help them make such decisions.

The text is in two parts. The first covers the mechanics of rendering character-based Japanese in an English environment. The second part looks at the various stylistic decisions that need to be made to insure clarity and consistency. Throughout we provide highlighted "recommendations" for those in need of a safe, quick, simply stated rule. Bear in mind, however, that each publication needs to be considered on its own terms. Stylistic "rules" generally need a certain amount of fine-tuning.

In the Appendices are useful guides to areas that are typically problematic, including periodization and era-name dating, geography, and converting Japanese measurements and large numbers into their Western equivalents. Translators and scholars in need of specialized information should consult more comprehensive sources such as those suggested in **Further References**.

As an organization of professionals working with the English language in Japan, SWET hopes this guide will help our colleagues working in many countries and genres to make informed choices and to set high editorial standards for their publications.

Society of Writers, Editors and Translators
Tokyo, Japan

Tips for the Nonspecialist

··

If having specialized knowledge about Japan is not a part of your job description, this brief introductory section is for you. You may be an editor at a book publisher or a fact-checker at a newspaper. Suddenly, you are handed a manuscript about Japan. . . . Is the material accurate? If not, where do you go for good information? How do you assess it in the first place? A few general guidelines:

- Rendering Japanese words in the letters of the Latin alphabet is called *romanization*. Japanese romanization rules are strict but simple. Look at the romanization chart in the Appendices. Then page through your manuscript. If you see irregular letter usage in any of its romanized Japanese, chances are your author is wrong about other things too, especially anything that pertains to language.

- That your text has been looked over by a "native speaker of Japanese" is not necessarily a guarantee of quality or accuracy. If the native speaker is not an expert in the subject area of your manuscript, it might be advisable to have the text rechecked. You may be able to find your own "expert" at a local university. The reference works cited at the end of this book are invaluable sources of information.

- Some Japanese conventions are very different from those used in the West. Be especially diligent when dealing with names of people, street addresses, and large numbers, especially those over 10,000.

Specialized Terms for Japan-Related Text

The following terms come up frequently in any discussion of editing romanized, Japan-related text.

macron: a diacritical mark ("long mark") used above a Japanese vowel when romanized to indicate an extended vowel sound: *â, î, ū, ê, ō*. Macrons are considered optional by many writers and editors, but they are the most accurate way of indicating correct pronunciation.

rōmaji: the Japanese term for the roman letters used to transliterate the sounds of Japanese in English.

kana: the two phonetic syllabaries—*hiragana* and *katakana*—used to write all the sounds in modern Japanese. Because *katakana* is used for words adopted from other languages, it includes some orthography not seen in *hiragana*.

kanji: Japanese characters used in combination with *kana* to write modern Japanese texts. There are over 2,000 *kanji* in common use. How a *kanji* is read (pronounced) depends on context and convention and cannot always be predicted. *Kanji* have more than one reading: readings derived from Chinese pronunciation (*on*) and those derived from native Japanese vocabulary (*kun*).

furigana: small syllabic *kana* characters placed above or beside *kanji* in running text to indicate correct pronunciation. *Furigana* are often used with proper names, variant or nonstandard readings, and unusual or rarely used *kanji*. Editors with access to Japanese sources frequently rely on *furigana* to check romanization.

ROMAN TYPE VS. ROMANIZATION

To avoid confusion with the word "romanization," in this book we use the phrase "normal-style type" to indicate what would otherwise be called "roman"—that is, non-italicized type.

Transliterating Japanese

Editing English-language texts that include Japanese words requires a certain amount of technical knowledge about romanization. There are two major systems of romanization in use today—Hepburn and Kunrei—with scattered exceptions and words that are still spelled in archaic romanized forms. This section explains these systems, how they are used, and how to "finetune" them for specialized or general material.

Skillful editing of Japanese words in English texts involves both flexible use of available rules and knowledge of the practices appropriate for a particular subject-matter or genre of writing. One set of rules may be preferred for texts in art history, another for writing in the social sciences, and yet another for international news or sports writing. Editors, authors, designers, and typographers must also consult with each other to coordinate their preferences and requirements.

Careful and consistent romanization is particularly desirable in specialized or scholarly writings about Japan. Accurate transcription of bibliographical data for Japanese references, for example, makes it possible for readers to locate works for further research without the aid of the original Japanese characters. For this reason, editors of Japan-related works may decide to use macrons to mark long or extended vowels, to insert apostrophes to aid correct syllabification, and to exercise extra care with hyphens and word division.

The phonetic units from which Japanese words are composed are limited in number, so romanization is not particularly difficult for a person who knows at least the rudiments of the lan-

USING KANJI IN ENGLISH TEXT

Except in specialized publications it is generally unnecessary to use actual Japanese characters (*kanji*) instead of their romanized equivalents. *Kanji* may be used in text discussions pertaining to language, of course, or in bibliographies intended for researchers. In running text, *kanji* should appear immediately after the words or titles they correspond to.

With most manuscripts now prepared electronically, the use of Japanese characters in English text presents various technical problems, among them coding, screen display, output, and stripping into final film (if film is used at all). Editors and writers should first ask themselves whether the use of *kanji* is essential to the presentation. If it is, they should be sure to work closely with the production staff to avoid delays and additional costs.

guage. However, a text heavily laden with, for example, place names, personal names, technical terms, and bibliographical data can present unexpected problems.

ROMANIZATION SYSTEMS

- **Use the Hepburn romanization system to transliterate Japanese words.**
- **Respect established variants.**

Hepburn System

TABLE OF THE HEPBURN SYSTEM

A table showing the complete Hepburn system of romanization appears on pages 50–51 in the Appendices.

Also called the Hyōjun system, the Hepburn system (Hebonshiki) is the most widely used method of romanization. It was named after James C. Hepburn, the nineteenth-century American missionary, and propagated through his *Japanese and English Dictionary* (1867). Based on English consonants and Italian and German vowels, the Hepburn system is used by all the major English-language publishers, academic presses, journals, and newspapers that work closely with Japan or Japanese topics. It is the system employed by all the Japanese-English dictionaries with romanized entries. The reason, which we support, is that it provides the closest approximation to accurate pronunciation of Japanese for the general English reader.

Kunrei System

Adopted as the official romanization system of Japan in 1937, the Kunrei system is taught in Japanese schools and is used by the National Diet Library. Advocates believe it best reflects the phonemic structure of Japanese, but it is rarely seen in publications.

Nippon System

The Nippon romanization system, predating Kunrei, was used mainly in the prewar period. Its main differences from the Kunrei system are the use of *kwa* for *ka*, *gwa* for *ga*, and *wo* for *o*.

Common Variants

Editors may see variant romanizations used in certain words and proper names that reflect historical convention or a particular individual's personal preference. In these cases, the variant may be used regardless of the romanization system used elsewhere in the publication.

HEPBURN ROMANIZATION	KNOWN VARIANT
Chichibu (mountains)	Titibu
en	yen
Inoue	Inouye
Kansai Gakuin University	Kwansai Gakuin University
Mt. Fuji	Mt. Huzi
Itō	Itoh
Reiko	Leiko
Suzuki Daisetsu	Suzuki Daisetz
kaidan	Kwaidan *(title of English publication by Lafcadio Hearn)*

SCHOLARLY PRACTICE

In academic publications, editors often choose to advise readers as to the romanization system used throughout and any special variants or exceptions. This note generally belongs in the author's or translator's preface, but it can appear at the first instance of a Japanese word in the text or even on the copyright page.

LONG VOWELS

- Use macrons to represent long vowels in publications for specialists, or when the words are important in a linguistic sense.

- Macrons can be omitted in general material or when using them creates proofreading or production problems.

Japanese phonetics are relatively simple, with five vowels (*a, i, u, e,* and *o*) that can be pronounced short or long. How to handle long vowels is an editorial decision, the crux of which is: Should you indicate long vowels or ignore them?

Macrons: Long Marks

Macrons are bars over vowels that indicate a long vowel (that is, sounded longer; the actual vowel sound of a long vowel is the same as its corresponding short form). In English texts, macrons make it easier to determine, for example, whether a word means "bird" (*tori*) or "street" (*tōri*). Because the Hepburn system favors their use for encouraging correct pronunciation, macrons are widely found in publications where this is a concern of authors and readers, mainly in books in the social sciences and humanities, journals and newsletters oriented to Japan specialists, and writings on culture and the arts for people with specialized interests. In lists of references in a scholarly work it is especially helpful to have macrons included.

Shujin no shōmei (*The Husband's Testimony*)
Shūjin no shōmei (*The Prisoner's Testimony*)

Edo no kozō (*Boys of Edo*)

Edo no kōzō (*The Structure of Edo*)

Nihon shoseki sōmokuroku (*Comprehensive Catalog of Japanese Books*)

Nihon shōseki sōmokuroku (*Comprehensive Catalog of Japanese Evidence*)

O and *u* are the most commonly found long vowels in Japanese. In loanwords, however, any vowel can be elongated.

bīru	*beer* [*but* biru (*building*)]
konpyūtā	*computer*
bēsubōru	*baseball*
Māfi no hōsoku	*Murphy's law*

Arguments in Favor of Macrons

A macron, though it may be unfamiliar to English speakers, distinguishes different sounds in Japanese and encourages more accurate pronunciation of Japanese words.

There are many homonyms in Japanese, and there appear to be even more when the distinction between long and short vowels is not indicated. With careful use of macrons, the meaning of the romanized original is often clearer than without. For example, a best-selling book in 1993 was *Ōkami bugyō*. With the macron it is fairly clear that the meaning of *ōkami* is "wolf"; without a macron, it might at first be confused with the word *okami*, which can mean either "officialdom" or "the wife/mistress/matron." This title was rendered as "The Wolf Town Commissioner." A book entitled *Rōjin* is definitely about "Old People," but one called *Rojin* could be about the Chinese writer Lu Xun.

Some Japanese words look like English words without a macron or other contrivance, as is the case with the name of

Since most digital fonts do not include macron characters, early stages of an electronic manuscript can be created with "dummy" characters as substitutes; circumflex or umlaut vowels are customary choices because they are rarely used in English text (but not never), resemble the macron itself (which makes proofreading easier), and have the same character widths as the characters they represent (thus avoiding copy reflow). When the text is reformatted during layout, the digital font with macrons replaces the earlier font. If the final production font has been cloned so that its macron characters correspond to the dummy characters in the original font, all the macrons should automatically be swapped in and appear in their proper places in the text. Authors and editors working at an early stage should decide (in consultation with the typesetter) which characters are to serve as macron dummies.

Note that a modified font is still copyrighted. You may not sell or distribute a font you have edited without the permission of the original font manufacturer.

Japan's classical theater, which can be transcribed No, Nō, Noh, *nō,* or *noh,* but preferably not simply "no."

Arguments against Macrons

Some publishers of newspapers and many magazines, even those that deal specifically with Japan, do not use macrons, believing that they confuse or alienate readers. Another consideration is that macrons must be used consistently—always or never—and it may be difficult to check or query every unfamiliar term. Also figuring in the decision are extra costs, typesetting difficulties, and proofreading problems. If readers' interest in pronouncing Japanese words is minimal, the trouble it takes to make sure all the macrons are present, and in the right places, may seem wasted. This is usually the case for texts in which most romanized Japanese is avoided in the first place because of the difficulties it creates for the nonspecialist.

Technical Considerations of Macron Use

Because macron-marked vowels like $\bar{o}$ and $\bar{u}$ are not widely available in typesetting and word-processing hardware or software, they can be especially troublesome to keyboard, specify, and transfer from one output medium to another. Authors preparing electronic manuscripts sometimes insert macrons using awkward superscript/backspace keyboard combinations; old-style typesetting systems can be just as cumbersome. With rapid advances in digital type, however, problems of cost and of fonts lacking characters with macrons will eventually disappear. Indeed, an off-the-shelf development tool like Fontographer can produce a fully macronized font family in less than an hour. Editors should check with those responsible for production at an early stage, and writers should coordinate manuscript preparation with their editors to avoid problems and delays caused by macron usage.

Other Long-Vowel Markers

The Circumflex

Instead of the awkward macron, the circumflex is often used by those with typewriters or who need some quick and easy way to indicate long vowels. A circumflex is defined by Webster's as "a mark . . . used in Greek over long vowels to indicate a rising-falling tone and in other languages to mark length, contraction, or a particular vowel quality," so it cannot be called wrong usage, but many editors and specialists try to avoid it.

Hôryûji temple   bêsubôru

The circumflex can be used as a stand-in for the macron and then be digitally swapped out during layout.

Doubled Letters

As in the Kunrei system, a long vowel may be indicated by doubling the letter: *aa, ii, uu, ee, oo* (also seen as *ou*). This can be clumsy, however, if the word contains the same vowels in succession.

Takeno Jōō   *but* Takeno Joooo   *or* Takeno Jouou

Nonetheless, when long vowels are required and it is difficult to get satisfactory typographical results for macrons on *a*, *e*, or *i*, the doubled letter may be the best choice.

biiru (*beer*)   fantajii (*fantasy*)

erebeetaa (*elevator*)   raamen (*noodles*)

Oh, Oh

A solution to the long-vowel problem often adopted for *ō* is the use of *oh*, as in "Noh." (The romanization *uh* for *ū* is never seen, however.) Most frequently seen examples of *oh* are in names.

PURCHASING MACRON FONTS

Typefaces that come with macrons in place are available from:

Linguist's Software
P.O. Box 580
Edmonds, WA 98020
425-775-1130
fonts@linguistsoftware.com
www.linguistsoftware.com

See also **Internet Resources** for online sources of macron fonts.

MACRONS IN ANGLICIZED WORDS

Even in texts that use macrons, it is common practice to omit them in Japanese words fully acculturated in English, such as judo and sumo, and in widely known place names like Tokyo, Kyoto, Osaka, and Honshu. A partial list of anglicized Japanese words appears in the section **Italics** on page 31.

Ohmae Ken'ichi	Ōmae Ken'ichi
Ohoka Echizen no Kami	Ōoka Echizen no Kami
Andoh Tadao	Andō Tadao

DOES THE WORD HAVE A MACRON OR NOT?

Whether a word includes a long vowel or not can be ascertained using any reliable Japanese-English dictionary. See **Further References** in the Appendices. Texts in which macrons are used should be checked very carefully through the final proofreading stage, as consistency of usage is essential (and mistakes are easy to make). Proofreaders and editors should keep detailed style sheets to guard against the omission of macrons or their improper use in apparent homophones.

Some Japanese prefer this variant romanization, particularly if they are active internationally in business or journalism, because they feel the *oh* makes their names easier to pronounce. When citing a work published under a nonstandard romanization you should follow the original publication's style. When simply referring to a well-known Japanese individual who is widely known by a variant romanization, the choice is less easy, although our preference would be to offer the name in the form readers are likely to find most familiar. Many people of Japanese ancestry who live outside Japan also use variant spellings that of course must be adhered to, regardless of the system of romanization otherwise used throughout the work.

Long Vowels on the Internet

Doubled vowels are an acceptable solution in Internet correspondence, where e-mailed diacritical marks are often rendered as gibberish on the receiving end. But since e-mail is often of an informal nature, most writers don't bother to be precise and drop the macrons altogether (writing "Tookyoo" is just as confusing anyway). However, when using e-mail or e-mail attachments to submit edited, prepared text for publication, you should adopt a convention for displaying macrons that can be easily managed by a standard search-and-replace word processor function (use the code $o for ō, for example). Encoded binary files, which allow the transmission of text formats (boldface, italics, etc.) as well as special characters, may be the safer method when submitting files over the Internet; check with your intended recipient to avoid platform, encoding, and application incompatibilities.

N OR M:

SHINBUN OR SHIMBUN?

- **When romanizing the syllabic *n*, either *n* or *m* before *b*, *m*, or *p* is acceptable.**
- **Respect accepted variants.**

The only real debate on the Hepburn system involves the syllabic *n* before the consonant *b*, *m*, or *p*. Hepburn himself changed the *n* to an *m* to approximate the pronunciation of the original Japanese. This has given rise to two schools of romanization, one preferring the use of *n* and the other *m*. Opinion is evenly divided.

The N School

There is no syllabic *m* in Japanese; it is simply a matter of sound when pronounced. *N* users believe that being as faithful as possible to the syllabic *n* is the best policy. Thus they use

> shinbun genmai shinpai

Their cause is supported by Japanese-English dictionaries, including the authoritative *Kenkyusha*, all of which use *n*. Academic journals and writers in the social sciences tend to use *n*.

The M School

Hepburn does have a faithful following for the argument that the *m* is often closer to the actual Japanese pronunciation.

> shimbun gemmai shimpai

In some fields, such as art history, conventional use of the *m* is firmly established in words like Tempyō (the era in history) and Rimpa (the school of painting). Academics in the humanities—particularly in art and religion—and those who write on cultural topics tend to use the *m*.

Exceptions

Place Names

Note that there are place names and words whose romanizations have, through usage or sense, established themselves regardless of the hard and fast rules of the *n* and *m* schools.

Nihonbashi	*not*	Nihombashi
shuppanbutsu	*not*	shuppambutsu
kinenbi	*not*	kinembi
higanbana	*not*	higambana
senbazuru	*not*	sembazuru (*although this* is *seen*)

Especially in compound names and words like "Nihonbashi" (a Tokyo place name), *shuppanbutsu* ("published works"), and *kinenbi* ("commemoration day"), tinkering with a romanized spelling that has become well established is discouraged. (Note that using a hyphen in a compound like "Nihon-bashi" visually severs the *m*-sounding *n* from the following *b*; in this case, even in a document that prefers the *m*, the *n* can be safely used on the grounds of clarity and sense.)

Company Names

A number of companies or organizations prefer the use of *m* in their English names.

Asahi Shimbun   Toyo Keizai Shimposha

APOSTROPHES

> • **Use the apostrophe when the publication is for specialists or when precise word distinctions are important.**

While the apostrophe is used in English to indicate contraction of words or the possessive, in romanized Japanese it clarifies meaning and serves to make the division of syllables distinct.

Man'yōshū   Jōshin'etsu   Jun'ichirō

The apostrophe also helps avoid confusion in words that would otherwise look like homonyms. You can use an apostrophe after *n* when *n* is part of the preceding syllable and not the initial consonant in the following syllable.

chin'atsu (*oppression*)	*but*	Chinatsu (*a girl's name*)
kin'yū (*finance*)	*but*	kinyū (*write in*)
tan'i (*unit*)	*but*	tani (*valley*)
zen'i (*good will*)	*but*	zeni (*coin, money*)

Note that the question of apostrophe usage arises only when the following syllable begins with a *y* or a vowel. Two major dictionary publishers, *Kenkyusha* and *Sanseidō*, use apostrophes when necessary to indicate "when a vowel or *ya, yu,* or *yo* is preceded by an *n*."

When to Use the Apostrophe

Historians, scholarly publishers, librarians, and writers addressing "specialist" audiences—those whose professions require careful romanization—should use the apostrophe.

When Not to Use the Apostrophe

General writers and journalists may opt *not* to use the apostrophe, since such minute linguistic distinctions may not be understood and can be distracting to the reader. The apostrophe may also be dropped when there is no ready reference source for verifying correct usage.

When There Are Two Adjacent Vowels

Some writers and publications use an apostrophe or hyphen to separate two vowels.

Go'emon   go'on   Ni'imura

This should not be necessary, however, since the pronunciation of Japanese vowels is consistent.

DOUBLED "I" IN ADJECTIVES

The citation form of Japanese adjectives always ends in the letter *i*. When the preceding syllable also ends in *i* (most often the syllable *shi*), the result is a word ending in *ii*. A macron should never be used over a single *i* in this case. Nor should the *ii* be written as *i'i*.

oishii   kibishii

HYPHENS

> • **Use hyphens sparingly.**
>
> • **Watch out for word division errors, especially in electronically set type.**

Hyphens are sometimes used to divide romanized words into meaningful units as an aid to understanding and pronunciation. But because the separation of words (i.e., morphological units) in Japanese is not always obvious, there have been no standard rules for using hyphens, and usage has been inconsistent. In the past, the hyphen was used quite frequently, as in

Hō-gaku-bu (*Faculty of Law*)

keizai-teki (*economic*)

Nanzen-ji (*temple name*)

shihon-shugi-shi (*history of capitalism*)

Today the editorial trend is toward eliminating the hyphen (perhaps reflecting the English move away from hyphens) wherever possible, opting instead for either two separate words or a single, unhyphenated word.

Hōgakubu

keizaiteki

Nanzenji

shihonshugishi *or* shihonshugi shi

In Common Nouns and Compounds

Writers and editors of materials in the social sciences, bibliographers, and librarians are constantly confronted with a plethora of short suffixes: *-teki, -gaku, -ron, -ka, -den, -shū,* and *-shi,* for example. To avoid unsightly type, suffixes to common nouns are best run together with their root words.

tensaiteki	kindaika	sekaishi
jinruigaku	eiyūden	ningenzō
shinkaron	mondaishū	sekaikan

When the root word is a proper noun or already a compound word, dividing the word with a space (instead of a hyphen) facilitates identification of the root.

Nihonjinron teki	Izumo no kuni	Chūgoku shi

Spaces should also be used when you need to divide up unmanageably long and unpronounceable terms into shorter meaningful units.

kaigai shinshutsu kigyō sōran
not   kaigai-shinshutsu-kigyō-sōran

In Personal Names

Hyphens should be used to set off honorific suffixes in personal names.

Watanabe-san (*Mr./Ms. Watanabe*)
Miyo-chan (*diminutive Miyo*)
Ikeda-kun (*young/junior/colleague Mr. Ikeda*)

For other status- or position-identifying terms, treat the suffix as a separate, capitalized word.

Tanaka Buchō (*Section Chief Tanaka*)
Koide Sensei (*teacher/master Koide*)
Minami Senpai (*senior colleague/schoolmate*)

In Place Names

Hyphens are often used to set off suffixes in place names, particularly when the suffix represents a formal geopolitical division.

Nagano-ken (*Nagano prefecture*)
Suginami-ku (*Suginami ward*)
Takamatsu-shi (*city of Takamatsu*)
Yamada-chō (*town of Yamada*)

There is much disagreement about the proper use of hyphens when writing out addresses. Take the following addresses, each of which can be transcribed three different ways:

Kami Kōya	Nishi Shinjuku	Shimo Ochiai
Kami-Kōya	Nishi-Shinjuku	Shimo-Ochiai
Kami-kōya	Nishi-shinjuku	Shimo-ochiai

JUN-ICHI OR JUN'ICHI?

The hyphen indicates a connection between two units of meaning, while the apostrophe is used as an aid to pronunciation. Thus, "Jun'ichi" is the correct romanized form of the personal name. Some individuals, however, may be sticklers regarding the use of hyphens in their own names. Especially if they have been published with that usage before, you should honor their preferred spellings, even at the expense of consistency.

In these cases, geographical considerations as well as typographical preferences can help you decide which form to use. If you don't like hyphens, avoid them. If there is a Kami ("upper") and a Shimo ("lower") pair of districts, the "Kami" is clearly a prefix and the hyphen can be justified. If "Kamikōya" is clearly one word in local parlance, no doubt the hyphen is artificial. Whether to use a hyphen with the often-seen *chō* or *machi* (a suffix denoting a village or small district) is up to personal preference. There are no hard and fast rules. *Be consistent.* For more about place names and addresses, see the section **Place Names**.

Vernacular Style

You can safely dispense with hyphens in place names with suffixes—such as temple names, mountains, and rivers—expressed in vernacular style unless there is reason to call attention to the suffix.

> Hasedera   Tōdaiji   Asamayama   Yodogawa

One reason for this is that these words are not considered divisible. "Tōdai temple," for example, is so rarely heard and sounds so odd that it might be considered a temple different from the famous religious complex in Nara. Hasedera, also, is a proper name in and of itself; we would not say "Hase temple." Names of mountains and rivers in the local vernacular would be expressed as one word: Fujisan, Asamayama, Yodogawa. A more international approach might be to call them Mt. Fuji, Mt. Asama, the Yodo River.

With Country-Name Compounds

Romanization is tricky when treaties or relationships between two countries are referred to, since Japanese writers often employ single-character combining forms like Nichi (from Nihon) for

Japan, Bei (Beikoku) for the United States, Chū (Chūgoku) for China, and so on. Usually the romanized syllables denoting each country can be put side by side separated by a hyphen or en dash, but in some compounds editors dispense with the dash to reflect the pronunciation of the combined form in Japanese.

Nichi-Bei *(Japan–U.S.)*   Nit-Chū/Nitchū *(Japan–China)*
Nichi-Ō *(Japan-Europe)*   Nis-Sō/Nissō *(Japan–Soviet)*

Word Division

Computerized typesetting often produces unacceptable word divisions in romanized Japanese. Extra care must be taken in proofreading. If a place name, personal name, or other Japanese word must be divided at the end of a line, the ideal place to divide is between the elements (*kanji* characters) used to write the word in the original Japanese. For example, in the case of the city name Matsuyama, written with two characters ("pine" + "mountain"), this would mean dividing the word as Matsu/yama.

Most Japanese syllables end with a vowel; the rest end with *n* as in the word "Shinkansen." When Japanese words are very long and space is limited, or if you are unfamiliar with the characters, the rule of thumb is to divide after a vowel or after the syllabic *n*, according to the Japanese syllabary.

Ma/tsu/ya/ma   Shin/kan/sen

A division to be avoided, therefore, is Mat/suyama (see sidebar). Japanese syllables can be determined using the Hepburn romanization chart on pages 50–51.

HYPHENATION HELP

The algorithms used in most word processing and DTP programs invariably break the syllable *tsu* in the wrong place: *mat-su* instead of *ma-tsu*, Once text is set in type be sure to recheck all line endings for errors. To speed the process, add frequently used words to your custom hyphenation dictionaries. Also note the following:

Ja-pan
but
Japa-nese

Many experienced editors assiduously avoid the potentially offensive "Jap-" at the end of a line, although according to most dictionaries and spelling guides such hyphenation is permissible.

Matters of Style

Compared with the relatively straightforward rules for transliterating Japanese, the guidelines for the handling of Japanese words as part of English text are by no means absolute. Each writer or editor must create a style matrix for each publication based on the readership, preferences of the author(s), and content. This section outlines the options that writers and editors can draw on in making style decisions, particularly for notation of long vowels (whether to mark or ignore), for italicization, and for name order (Japanese or Western).

Style decisions must of course be made with a realistic appraisal of the situation. If macrons are going to be used, is the author available to check them? If all Japanese terms are italicized every time, will the pages be littered with words in italics? If Western name order is adopted, what happens when the name of a historical figure like Toyotomi Hideyoshi crops up?

Do you want a style that emphasizes the specialized nature of the material or deemphasizes it? For example, a newspaper article about current business trends in Japan might talk about "keiretsu," "kanban" systems, and "Kayabacho" as if these words were an accepted part of the English language. A scholarly book about the history of management practices might require the use of stricter notation, italicizing the first two nouns and adding a macron to the third word, a place name: Kayabachō.

Many Japanese words are already part of the English language, others are borderline, and the rest are still considered foreign. The following sections can help you decide where to draw the line between romanization and English, how to decide whether certain words are proper nouns, and how to handle plurals and other copyediting minutiae.

ITALICS

> • **In general apply the rules of italicization in English.**
>
> • **Italicize all Japanese words except those that have been anglicized. After its first appearance, an italicized Japanese word that appears frequently in the text can be set in normal-style type.**

General Rules for Italicization

In general, apply the rules of italicization used for English (see *The Chicago Manual of Style*). Titles of books, periodicals, and other published materials should be italicized.

CLASSICS: *Taiheiki, Man'yōshū*

CONTEMPORARY BOOKS: *No! to ieru Nihon*

MAGAZINES: *Bungei shunjū*

OTHER PUBLICATIONS: *Keizai hakusho*

Proper nouns (i.e., names of persons, places, families, organizations, institutions, schools of thought or art, or eras) are usually *not* italicized—except when used in a generic sense.

PERSONAL NAMES: Morita Akio, Murasaki Shikibu, Misora Hibari

PLACE NAMES: Tōhoku, Suemura, Enoshima, Chūbu region

FAMILY NAMES: Tachibana, Fujita, Kikuchi, Miyamoto

SCHOOLS OF ART OR THOUGHT: Kokugaku, Rimpa school, Urasenke

HISTORICAL ERAS AND PERIODS: Asuka, Sengoku, Kyōhō, Meiji, Heisei

ORGANIZATIONS: Fujin no Tomo no Kai, Keidanren, Toyota Zaidan, Koguma-za

Anglicized Words

Japanese words used in an English sentence are usually italicized, except for those that have entered the English language. (These anglicized words may, of course, still be italicized where desired for emphasis or when the content is very specialized.) The test of anglicization is appearance in the standard English-language dictionary of your choice. The selection of these loanwords differs from one dictionary to another, so in the end you must make a subjective judgment about whether the readers of a particular publication need the italic flag. Anglicized words do not use macrons; however, Japanese words set in normal-style type may use macrons or not. Here is a list of Japanese words commonly anglicized:

aikido	hiragana	koan	shiatsu
banzai	ikebana	koto	shogun
bonsai	jinrikisha	mikado	shoji
Bushido	judo	netsuke	soroban
daikon	jujitsu	Noh	sukiyaki
daimyo	kabuki	obi	sumo
geisha	kami	origami	sushi
genro	kanban	pachinko	tabi
haikai	karaoke	sake	tanka
haiku	karate	samisen	tatami
haori	keiretsu	samurai	ukiyo-e
harakiri	kendo	sashimi	zaibatsu
hibachi	kimono	shakuhachi	zori

EDITING SPECIALIZED CONTENT

When working on a specialized text, you may come across some words that are very well known in the West and others that are hardly known at all. For example, a text on Japanese poetry might mix common and uncommon terms like *haiku, tanka, renga, renku, waka, haikai, kyoka,* and so on. You may italicize all the Japanese words, none of them, or only those that are not in your English dictionary of choice.

Style Options for Italicization

Having decided which words to treat as English and which to treat as Japanese, the editor or writer must next select a style that will govern how italics will be used in the text. There are three main options.

Italicize Each Japanese Word Every Time

Italicizing Japanese words every time they occur coincides with standard usage and has the advantage of consistency; the reader needs no explanation. A drawback is that in texts where such words appear frequently, the page may become overly laden with italics, detracting from the design of the publication.

Italicize Nothing

While less popular with editors and readers, not using italics may be more agreeable to some designers. If a Japanese term is defined on its first appearance in the text, it can be used throughout the rest of the publication like a specialized English term. If there are many such terms in a lengthy text, a glossary is a useful support for the reader. This no-italics system is not recommended for publications whose readers cannot be expected to be familiar with Japanese terms.

Italicize on First Appearance Only

The compromise between the two systems above is to italicize a word on first appearance only and not thereafter. (In an anthology, particularly one with contributions by many authors, this method may be modified to cover the first appearance within each chapter.) First-word-only italicization eliminates the problem of excessive italics in a text and is preferred by a number of publishers and journals whose readers are assumed to have special inter-

---

AVOIDING CONFUSION

In spite of the recognized anglicization of words like *nō* (as No or Noh) and *sake*, it is often a good idea to identify them in some way—by italicizing or, for instance, by placing an accent on the final *e* in saké—because they are so easily confused with other English words.

Note that "shogunate" is English, not Japanese, and should never be italicized. The same applies to "rickshaw" (the Japanese is *jinrikisha*) and "adzuki" (*azuki*) beans.

est in or knowledge about Japan. It can, however, be confusing to readers who are not reading a text straight through. And it requires a great deal of editorial diligence.

PERSONAL NAMES

> - **If possible, use Japanese name order: family name first, personal name last.**
>
> - **Be on the lookout for nonstandard readings of *kanji*.**
>
> - **Respect idiosyncratic romanized spellings.**

Name Order

Japanese write their names in their own language surname first, the same as Chinese and Koreans. After contact with the West was reestablished in the mid-nineteenth century, many Japanese adopted the practice of giving their surname last when dealing with foreigners. Japanese learn in school to reverse their names when writing or speaking in English. Japan's domestic English-language media follow this same practice, as do almost all non-Japanese media around the world. Especially in translations, either name order may be adopted. Writers and editors may also choose a hybrid approach.

Japanese Order: Surname, Personal Name

Readers who know Japan well often prefer to see Japanese names in their original order. Names can be written in customary Japanese order: surname first, personal name last.

ITALICS IN TITLES AND SUBHEADS

For design consistency, Japanese words normally italicized in a text can receive special handling when they appear in a title or subhead. For example, if an entire subhead is set in plain small caps, setting a Japanese word in italics might upset the look of the line (and italic forms may not be available for some display typefaces in any case).

Suzuki Zenkō   Mukai Chiaki   Ōe Kenzaburō

This practice is adopted by most scholarly publications in the humanities and social sciences and is consistent with contemporary treatment of Chinese and Korean names (e.g., Deng Xiao-ping and Kim Dae Jung). It also assures consistency throughout history: Fujiwara no Narihira, Ashikaga Takauji, Tokugawa Ieyasu, Itō Hirobumi, Nagai Kafū, Hosokawa Morihiro.

Western Order: Personal Name, Surname

You can give Japanese names following the common practice in the West (with the notable exception of Hungary): personal name first, surname last. There are several good reasons for handling names this way.

- Many Japanese active in the international arena since the Meiji period (1868–1912) have adopted the practice of switching their names around when dealing with foreigners to accommodate the assumptions of Westerners. Many Japanese prefer seeing their names in Western order when in a Western context.

- Since English-language news media like the *New York Times, Wall Street Journal,* and *Japan Times* consistently use Western order for contemporary Japanese figures, a reference to Prime Minister Hashimoto Ryūtarō may cause confusion.

- If the name of the author of a book or article is given in Japanese order, the name may appear reversed in library catalogs or other reference works compiled by someone not familiar with Japanese names. (In large alphabetical listings the mistaken placement of a work under a Japanese author's personal name—Kōbō instead of Abe, for example—can effectively "lose" the work entirely. A few publications give surnames in CAPS or SMALL CAPS to avoid this mix-up, but this is troublesome for the editor and wins no plaudits from designers or typesetters.)

- Since English readers assume that the second name given is the surname, no further explanation is necessary.

Western name order is particularly suitable for documents that rarely refer to historical figures, such as newspapers, magazines, and conference papers on current international affairs, science, technology, advertising, business, and so on.

The disadvantage of using Western order is discovered when pre-Meiji historical or literary figures are mentioned. Reversing the names of well-known and important people like Toyotomi Hideyoshi, Katsu Kaishū, and Sen no Rikyū sounds very odd (as odd as Shakespeare William or Da Gama Vasco).

Pre-Meiji Japanese, Post-Meiji Western

You can adopt a hybrid approach. For Meiji and post-Meiji (that is, post-1868) figures, use Western order; for pre-Meiji figures, use traditional Japanese order. Always make a point of explaining this practice in a preface or in a footnote on the first appearance of a name. This mixed method has been used by several leading publishers in Japan. However, inevitably there appears a historical figure whose prominence spans the pre- and post-Meiji years—for example, Saigō Takamori (1827–77) or Takasugi Shinsaku (1839–67). In such a case you simply have to choose.

A variation on the hybrid approach is to use Japanese name order in publications on Japan's literature, history, or culture (regardless of the period) and Western name order in publications in other disciplines, such as economics, geology, or medicine. The idea here is that readers of the former type of publication are accustomed to Japanese order—and would even be put off by use of Western order—while those of the latter type are more comfortable with Western order.

Our Recommendation

The decision on which style to adopt must be made with the readers of your publication in mind. We encourage use of Japanese name order—family name first, personal name last—on the principle that, notwithstanding the willingness of Meiji leaders to accommodate the West, Japanese should be as free as Chinese and Koreans to use their names in customary order.

Common Problems with Japanese Names

Editors and translators of specialized works, particularly in history, the arts, and literature, face many difficulties when working with Japanese names. Several of the most problematic name-related issues are addressed here.

Pseudonyms and Art Names

For historical personages, dictionaries like Kadokawa Shoten"s *Nihonshi jiten* give correct readings of names and can also be helpful in sorting out the pseudonyms and "art" names used extensively in pre-twentieth-century Japan.

An art name is a bit like a pen name; it is generally a personal name adopted by or bestowed on an artist or writer and becomes the name by which he is known in the art or literary world. For example, the late-Meiji writer Natsume Sōseki's art name is Sōseki, so he is referred to on second mention as Sōseki, even though his family name is Natsume. Mori Ōgai and Shimazaki Tōson are other examples, referred to respectively by their art names Ōgai and Tōson. The writer Kawabata Yasunari used his birth name, so he is referred to as Kawabata. Novelist Mishima

---

NAMES IN BACKMATTER

Compiling indexes and bibliographies also requires special attention to name order. Be sure to follow the same style used in the main text, and be aware that, as such material is often compiled from various different sources, inconsistencies may have slipped into the final manuscript. Double-check all names to be sure. See also the section **Note, Bibliography, and Index Styles**.

Yukio used a pseudonym, so the writer is referred to as Mishima. The use of art names, while unavoidable, can be confusing when the rule of adhering strictly to Japanese name order is adopted and readers are not familiar with how certain persons are customarily referred to.

Variant Readings

Japanese personal names, written in characters for which there are often variant readings, present translators with many difficulties. Characters used in names can be unusual and obscure, or their readings—for historical or other reasons—sometimes differ from those customarily used in standard texts. However, each individual's name has only *one* correct reading, and reliable sources should be checked to ascertain it. Also, care should be taken to always give the correct *contextual* reading; checking in a dictionary and finding the reading of a particular character does not guarantee that that character is read the same way when used in a particular personal name.

Different reference works sometimes give different readings for the same names. Good Japanese sources include *Concise Nihon jinmei jiten* (Concise dictionary of Japanese names) and *Saikin choshamei yomikata jiten* (Reading dictionary of recent author names). See **Further References** for more information on these works. Editors should always query authors about their sources to make sure their transcriptions are reliable.

Imperial Names

Members of the Japanese imperial family have two names: (1) names that are used during their lifetimes and (2) posthumous titles. The emperor of Japan from 1926 to 1989 was Hirohito. Since his death he has been known as the Shōwa Emperor or Emperor Shōwa (the period of his reign was called the Shōwa period during his lifetime, and that name has not changed). For a complete listing of imperial and era names, see the tables in the Appendices.

Clan Names

Japan's ancient aristocracy consisted of a limited number of clans (*uji*; e.g., Fujiwara, Taira), so the "family name" alone is inadequate to denote clan members. The clan name and given name should be connected with *no*.

> Fujiwara no Teika   Kamo no Mabuchi   Ono no Komachi

The same practice is sometimes used to denote art lineages.

> Sen no Rikyū   Ike no Taiga

Personal Variants

For present-day names, a person's preference for the romanized spelling of his or her name should always be respected, even when it differs from your romanization of choice.

ACCEPTABLE VARIANT	IF STANDARD HEPBURN
Kenichi Ohmae	Ōmae Ken'ichi
Akira Iriye	Irie Akira
Shidzue Katō	Katō Shizue
Jun-ichi Kyogoku	Kyōgoku Jun'ichi

Whenever possible, check with the individual in question.

PLACE NAMES

> - Either transliterate or translate place-name suffixes.
>
> - Retain Japanese suffixes that are an established part of the place name.
>
> - Beware of transcription and consistency errors when working with Japanese street addresses.

Descriptive Suffixes

Japanese place names, especially for administrative units, often include a descriptive suffix. For example, Tōkyō-to is, literally, "Tokyo Metropolis," and *-to* is an official administrative category. Hinohara-mura is, literally, "Hinohara village," *-mura* meaning "village."

Descriptive suffixes are also used for major topographical features such as rivers and mountains: Sumida-gawa (*-gawa* means "river") and Fuji-san (*-san* means "mountain"). Regarding the use of hyphens in these terms, see the section **Hyphens**.

There are three methods for handling these suffixes.

Transliterate the Suffix

Place names can be simply transliterated (romanized).

> Setagaya-ku (*Setagaya is one of Tokyo's 23 wards*)
>
> Ōita-ken (*-ken is "prefecture"*)
>
> Yamanote-sen (*-sen is "line," as in train or subway line*)
>
> Setonaikai (*-nai is "inland" and -kai is "sea"*)
>
> Sumida-gawa (*-gawa is "river"*)
>
> Heian Jingū (*a jingū is a large head shrine*)
>
> Tōdaiji (*-ji is "temple"*)
>
> Chūō-dōri (*-dōri is "avenue"*)

TEMPLE SUFFIXES

The character that acts as a suffix to indicate the name of a Buddhist temple can be read *-ji* or *-tera/dera*, depending on whether the Chinese- or Japanese-style reading is used. This is determined by convention, and editors and writers should try in all cases to follow customary usage.

Mashuko (ko *is "lake"*)

Tōmei Kōsoku Dōro (kōsoku dōro *is "expressway"*)

Hakkōda-san (-san *is "mountain"*)

This system may be preferred because such names sound "right" to people who know Japan well and enable a reader, for example, to ask directions to a place using the Japanese word. Its disadvantage is that the *-ji, -gawa,* and so on do not communicate meaning to persons who do not know Japanese and will be considered part of the proper noun.

To clarify the meaning, some writers tack an English geographical term onto the Japanese, rendering Shiga-san as "Mt. Shiga-san" or Biwako as "Lake Biwako." This is obviously redundant and represents an unnecessary attachment to the original Japanese. Just as we say Mt. Fuji, we can say Mt. Shiga, Mr. Tanaka (Tanaka-san), or Professor Suzuki (Suzuki Sensei).

Translate the Suffix

You can leave out the Japanese suffixes that describe the place; instead, use the English equivalents.

Setagaya Ward	Ōita Prefecture
Yamanote Line	Tōdai Temple
Chūō Avenue	Tōmei Expressway
Mt. Fuji	Nihon Bridge

VARIANTS IN READINGS

Correct readings of place names (either in *rōmaji* or *kana)* can be found in many atlases published in Japan—but be prepared for differences in readings (Ibaraki/Ibaragi), even in Japanese. Be sure to check for the correct reading. (See **Further References** in the Appendices.)

This method is often used by newspapers like the *Japan Times.* The major problem here is that some place names become unrecognizable or confusing without the suffix: "Nihon Bridge" does not immediately bring the word "Nihonbashi" to mind, especially if one is referring to the well-known Nihonbashi area of Tokyo.

Transliterate and Explain

You can also solve the recognition problem by combining the two methods above: Keep the Japanese place name intact and add a word of explanation at least on first mention, e.g., "Nihonbashi bridge" or "Tōdaiji temple," despite the redundancy. Using a lower-case noun is preferable to uppercase ("Tōdaiji Temple"), which would make the redundancy all the more noticeable. A better approach is to introduce the term with a broader, descriptive definition: Ryōanji might be introduced first as "the famous Kyoto temple Ryōanji," and then given as "Ryōanji" thereafter.

Styles for Japanese Addresses

Administrative Divisions

In English, Japan's forty-seven administrative divisions are called prefectures; in Japanese, however, these represent four different types of unit: *to, dō, fu,* and *ken* (capital, territory, metropolis, and prefecture). Tokyo is a *to*—the capital; the entire island of Hokkaido is a *dō*—a territory; Osaka and Kyoto, which both encompass much more than the cities of the same names, are *fu*—they are chiefly metropolitan prefectures; the other forty-three are ordinary prefectures. The main local government units are:

shi	*city; municipality*
machi (*or* chō)	*town*
mura (*or* son)	*village; township*

A *shi* centers on a city and embraces outlying suburbs that may be very rural. A *machi* (the same character can also be read *chō*), is an internal municipal unit; despite the name it may be quite rural. *Mura* is especially tricky, since it can mean literally "village," as in "a cluster of dwellings," as well as a large administrative unit resembling a township. Within such a village-type *mura*, one often finds *buraku* or "hamlets"—clusters of dwellings—separated by fields or mountains.

WHEN TO USE THE WORD "PREFECTURE"

Although Kyoto and Osaka are *fu*, it is possible in English to refer to them as prefectures (normally indicated by the suffix *-ken*). Hokkaido and Tokyo are almost never referred to as prefectures, however.

Address-Line Sequence

Street addresses in Japanese publications are customarily given in order of large to small (prefecture, city, block area, block subsection, house number, name of addressee). This is the reverse of Western address-line sequence (name, street, city, state). When Japanese addresses are presented in English texts, all the elements thus need to be reversed.

JAPANESE ORDER	WESTERN ORDER
Japan	Fujimichi Hanae
Hiroshima 722-0011	Sakura-machi 1-2-79
Onomichi-shi	Onomichi-shi
Sakura-machi 1-2-79	Hiroshima 722-0011
Fujimichi Hanae	Japan

This reversal often occasions transcription errors. Editors and writers should be sure to double-check all Japanese street addresses for consistency of sequence. The following are important points:

- The postal code (as of February 1998) consists of seven digits and is placed after the prefecture name.

- Some cities and prefectures have the same name. Chiba City is in Chiba Prefecture. Thus, addresses that end "Chiba, Chiba 260-0852" are not necessarily incorrect.

- The local portion of the street address can be given in either of two ways in English.

  (A)   1-2-70 Sakura-machi
  (B)   2-70 Sakura-machi, 1-chōme

Both address lines refer to the 70th building in the 2nd subsection of the 1st block area (*chōme*) of the district Sakura-machi. Style A is the way it appears in most

USE SHORT FORMS

It is administrative practice in many government offices in Japan to translate all municipalities as XXX City or YYY Town because every administrative unit has an official designation: *shi* (city), *machi* (town), *mura* (township, village), etc. In English, the name of the place alone should suffice: Maebashi, rather than Maebashi City; Tokyo, rather than Tokyo Metropolis; Hachiōji, rather than Hachiōji City. In some contexts, the phrasing "city of Maebashi" or "in the city Maebashi" may be desirable.

English-language listings in Japan. Style B is often rec-ommended for English inscription by the Japanese post office. Many English-language editors prefer style A, however, because it is shorter and because there is less room for error when translating from Japanese sources. Style B provides a bit more information for the traveler. Either is correct, but both styles should not be used in the same publication.

• Many Japanese commercial buildings and apartment houses have names that include "exotic" non-Japanese terms like *heights, maison, casa, plaza,* and so on. When transcribing these addresses in English text, you should in most cases use the original non-Japanese spelling of the word instead of the less-than-obvious romanization of the Japanese. See also **Loanwords**.

CAPITALIZATION

> • **Follow English style; capitalize as little as possible.**

Since written Japanese makes no distinction between upper- and lowercase, your rules for capitalization can follow the same stan-dards used for English: capitalize as little as possible—only per-sonal names, official titles, and names of places and institutions, as prescribed by *The Chicago Manual of Style* and other style guides.

An exception often made in romanized Japanese is that names of artistic or performing arts—Noh, Kabuki, Bunraku, Jōruri, Kiyomoto, Shingeki—are capitalized when they are not italicized. As institutionalized genres, they are in one sense proper nouns, but in another sense they are ordinary genres; in fact "kabuki" is in the English dictionary as a lowercase noun, and it can refer not only to the urban nationally supported kabuki of Tokyo and Osaka but to folk or country theater as well.

For a discussion of capitalization as applied to book and article titles, see **Note, Bibliography, and Index Styles**.

PLURALS

> • **Let the same romanized Japanese word serve for both singular and plural forms.**

Most Japanese nouns are in a form that can be either singular or plural, so the writer or editor must decide what to do about plural forms of Japanese words used in an English sentence.

> Ryōkan wrote three *renga*s during this period.
>
> Ryōkan wrote three *renga* during this period.

We advise leaving Japanese words in singular form, regardless of whether the word is italicized to indicate a foreign word or treated as an anglicized word in regular type.

three genro	*not*	three genros
three kimono	*not*	three kimonos

Chinese publishers are rapidly translating *manga* for a thirsty domestic readership.

Keiretsu all over Japan are being challenged by companies from overseas.

AVOID THE ITALIC "S"

We don't recommend making Japanese nouns plural (see discussion on this page). But if for some reason you do, be sure the final *s* that indicates the plural is not italicized along with the Japanese word:

*tokonoma*s *roji*s

The mixing of type styles in a single word is profoundly unattractive—all the more reason to avoid using the *s* in the first place.

LOANWORDS

- **Except in bibliographic entries, use the original-language spelling of a foreign word when referring to publications and organizations.**

The Japanese language uses a large number of loanwords from other languages, particularly English. These loanwords are generally written in *katakana*, which effectively "Japanizes" the foreign word. For example, the term "part-time" in English is used frequently in Japan, where it is pronounced *pâto taimu*. (Some "loanwords" are purely Japanese inventions; e.g., *naitâ*, sports events that take place at night.)

When loanwords are used in the names of organizations and publications, they must sometimes be transliterated. An option here is to give the English spelling instead of the transliteration.

ROMANIZED JAPANESE	EQUIVALENT FOREIGN TERM
Ekonomisuto	*Economist*
Rikuruto	Recruit
Riburopoto	Libroport
Purejidentosha	President Sha

The advantage of anglicization is that the word will be instantly recognizable, whereas the Japanese version of a loanword can require puzzling out or result in awkward spellings. Use of the exact transliteration, however, does make it clear that it is a *Japanese* magazine called *Economist* that is is being talked about rather than the one published in English. In general, except when it is necessary to transliterate these loanwords exactly for bibliographic purposes, they should be given in their original forms.

NOTE, BIBLIOGRAPHY, AND INDEX STYLES

- **Use a "down" style for titles of Japanese works.**

- **Present Japanese names the same way as in the main text.**

Listing Japanese-language publications (books, magazine, and journal articles) in romanized form for a bibliography or references brings to the fore several of the style questions discussed in this book. For example:

- Capitalization: Should a book title follow the "down" style or the "up" style?

- Macrons: Is the publisher to be called Kōdansha or Kodansha? Chikuma Shobō or Chikuma Shobo?

- Word formation: Should a book on Shōwa history be rendered *Shōwa-shi, Shōwa shi, Shōwa Shi,* or *Shōwashi?*

These choices boil down to the same style decisions that must be made in assembling any English-language bibliography. The style followed in the publication determines the style followed in the backmatter. If macrons and hyphens are used in the text, they should be used in the notes, bibliography, and index as well.

Capitalization of Titles

The choice for presenting titles in a bibliographical list is essentially between the "up" style and "down" style.

The "up" style is the headline style that capitalizes all words except articles, prepositions, and conjunctions. The "down" style capitalizes only the first word and proper nouns.

The "down" style is recommended by *The Chicago Manual of Style*. We agree. Because it avoids the problem of having to decide what Japanese words are the "lowercase" equivalents of prepositions, articles, and conjunctions, it can be handled more easily by someone with no knowledge of Japanese.

> Kyōiku kōjō no kodomotachi (Children of the education factory)
>
> Tezuka Osamu no kimyō na sekai (The Curious World of Tezuka Osamu)

Translating Titles

The main purpose of providing bibliographic information is to enable readers to look things up. Therefore we recommend that the original Japanese title always be given, followed by a translation in parentheses or brackets; the translated title should appear in the "down" style and in normal-style type. If only the translated title is available, it may appear in the "up" style in italics, but be sure you provide information on the original language.

> Inose, Naoki. *Mikado no shōzō* (Portrait of the Mikado). Tokyo: Shinchōsha, 1986.
>
> Inose, Naoki. *Portrait of the Mikado* (in Japanese). Tokyo: Shinchōsha, 1986.

Publishers' Names

Use the romanized name and hyphenation preferred by the publisher where possible, even when the style is inconsistent with the text.

ITALICIZATION OF TITLES

Titles of Japanese works can be handled the same as titles in English: Use italics for names of books, and quoted normal-style type for titles of articles.

WHAT "BUNKO" MEANS

Occasionally one sees the word "Bunko" given as part of a publisher's name, but Bunko simply means "collection" or "series." The publisher of books under the imprint Iwanami Bunko is Iwanami Shoten. Similarly, the publisher of Shinchōbunko is, properly, Shinchōsha.

Kodansha International	*not* Kōdansha International
Chūō Kōron Sha	*not* Chūōkōronsha *or* Chūōkōron Sha
Shogakukan	*not* Shōgakkan

Note that some publishers, especially those with names derived from foreign words, have established English names.

Baseball Magazine-sha	Diamond, Inc.
Froebel-kan	Ohmsha
University of Tokyo Press	Ça et La Shobo

Authors' Names

The style used throughout the text for Japanese names should be followed in the notes and other backmatter. In the bibliography and index, if Japanese order is used in the main text, names are presented as is, family name first, with no comma between the family name and the personal name.

Morita Akio   Tsushima Yūko   Ota Hideaki

If Western order is used in the text, the Japanese name in the index is inverted and a comma added, as with a Western name:

Morita, Akio   Mishima, Yukio   Hashimoto, Ryūtarō

In the bibliography, as elsewhere, the writer or editor should be aware of the different ways of handling these items, select one that agrees with the tone and style of the rest of the publication, and watch out for inconsistencies.

Appendices

....

Hepburn Orthography

Prefectures, Provinces

Numbers

Units of Measure

Imperial Reigns and Historical Eras

Historical Eras, Alphabetical List

Modern Era Conversion Chart

Principal Periods of Japanese History

Further References

Internet Resources

SOUND CHANGES

The syllables *-chi* and *-tsu* can change their sounds when the following syllable begins with a consonant. This sometimes results in the following Hepburn spellings:

kk   Nikkō (ni-chi-ko-u)

pp   happō (ha-chi-po-u)

ss   bassuru (ba-tsu-su-ru)

tch   matcha (ma-tsu-cha)

tt   matte (ma-tsu-te)

Consonants in combination can also show sound shifts: *k* to *g*, *s* to *z*, *t* to *d*, and *h* to *b* or *p*. For example, *kawa* means "river," and the *k* changes to *g* in the compound Sumida-gawa, or "Sumida River."

HEPBURN ORTHOGRAPHY

The Hepburn system of transliterating Japanese words into a Western alphabet is used throughout the world. Words in the alternative Kunrei and Nippon systems can be respelled in Hepburn unless the alternative romanizations are well established or part of a bibliographical listing. *Hiragana* and *katakana* have the same character sets, but some *katakana* combinations used for "non-Japanese" sounds are almost never written in *hiragana*.

Simple Syllables

R	H	K	R	H	K	R	H	K	R	H	K	R	H	K
a	あ	ア	i	い	イ	u	う	ウ	e	え	エ	o	お	オ
ka	か	カ	ki	き	キ	ku	く	ク	ke	け	ケ	ko	こ	コ
sa	さ	サ	shi	し	シ	su	す	ス	se	せ	セ	so	そ	ソ
ta	た	タ	chi	ち	チ	tsu	つ	ツ	te	て	テ	to	と	ト
na	な	ナ	ni	に	ニ	nu	ぬ	ヌ	ne	ね	ネ	no	の	ノ
ha*	は	ハ	hi	ひ	ヒ	fu	ふ	フ	he†	へ	ヘ	ho	ほ	ホ
ma	ま	マ	mi	み	ミ	mu	む	ム	me	め	メ	mo	も	モ
ya	や	ヤ				yu	ゆ	ユ				yo	よ	ヨ
ra	ら	ラ	ri	り	リ	ru	る	ル	re	れ	レ	ro	ろ	ロ
wa	わ	ワ	wi‡	ゐ	ヰ				we‡	ゑ	ヱ	o#	を	ヲ
												nΔ	ん	ン

Voiced Consonants and "P"

ga	が	ガ	gi	ぎ	ギ	gu	ぐ	グ	ge	げ	ゲ	go	ご	ゴ
za	ざ	ザ	ji	じ	ジ	zu	ず	ズ	ze	ぜ	ゼ	zo	ぞ	ゾ
da	だ	ダ	ji	ぢ	ヂ	zu	づ	ヅ	de	で	デ	do	ど	ド
ba	ば	バ	bi	び	ビ	bu	ぶ	ブ	be	べ	ベ	bo	ぼ	ボ
pa	ぱ	パ	pi	ぴ	ピ	pu	ぷ	プ	pe	ぺ	ペ	po	ぽ	ポ

Short Compound Syllables

R	H	K	R	H	K	R	H	K
kya	きゃ	キャ	kyu	きゅ	キュ	kyo	きょ	キョ
sha	しゃ	シャ	shu	しゅ	シュ	sho	しょ	ショ
cha	ちゃ	チャ	chu	ちゅ	チュ	cho	ちょ	チョ
nya	にゃ	ニャ	nyu	にゅ	ニュ	nyo	にょ	ニョ
hya	ひゃ	ヒャ	hyu	ひゅ	ヒュ	hyo	ひょ	ヒョ
mya	みゃ	ミャ	myu	みゅ	ミュ	myo	みょ	ミョ
rya	りゃ	リャ	ryu	りゅ	リュ	ryo	りょ	リョ
gya	ぎゃ	ギャ	gyu	ぎゅ	ギュ	gyo	ぎょ	ギョ
ja	じゃ	ジャ	ju	じゅ	ジュ	jo	じょ	ジョ
ja	ぢゃ	ヂャ	ju	ぢゅ	ヂュ	jo	ぢょ	ヂョ
bya	びゃ	ビャ	byu	びゅ	ビュ	byo	びょ	ビョ
pya	ぴゃ	ピャ	pyu	ぴゅ	ピュ	pyo	ぴょ	ピョ

Long Compound Syllables

R	H	R	H	R	H	R	H
ū	うう	ō	おう				
kū	くう	kō	こう	kyū	きゅう	kyō	きょう
sū	すう	sō	そう	shū	しゅう	shō	しょう
tsū	つう	tō	とう	chū	ちゅう	chō	ちょう
nū	ぬう	nō	のう	nyū	にゅう	nyō	にょう
fū	ふう	hō	ほう	hyū	ひゅう	hyō	ひょう
mū	むう	mō	もう	myū	みゅう	myō	みょう
yū	ゆう	yō	よう				
rū	るう	rō	ろう	ryū	りゅう	ryō	りょう
gū	ぐう	gō	ごう	gyū	ぎゅう	gyō	ぎょう
zū	ずう	zō	ぞう	jū	じゅう	jō	じょう
zū	づう	zō	ぞう	jū	ぢゅう	jō	ぢょう
bū	ぶう	bō	ぼう	byū	びゅう	byō	びょう
pū	ぷう	pō	ぽう	pyū	ぴゅう	pyō	ぴょう

NON-HEPBURN SYSTEMS

Most Kunrei and Nippon romanizations are the same as Hepburn. Standard Kunrei and older Nippon variants (rarely seen) are

Hep	Kun	Nip	
ka	ka	kwa	
ga	ga	gwa	
shi	si	si	
ji	zi	zi	[voiced *shi*]
chi	ti	ti	
ji	zi	di	[voiced *chi*]
tsu	tu	tu	
zu	zu	du	[voiced *tsu*]
fu	hu	hu	
o	o	wo	

Kunrei/Nippon variants for compound syllables are

Hep	Kun	Nip
sha	sya	sya
shu	syu	syu
sho	syo	syo
[voiced *sha*...]		
ja	zya	zya
ju	zyu	zyu
jo	zyo	zyo
cha	tya	tya
chu	tyu	tyu
cho	tyo	tyo
[voiced *cha*...]		
ja	zya	dya
ju	zyu	dyu
jo	zyo	dyo

PREFECTURES, PROVINCES

Prefectures

NOTE

Proper names on this and the facing page appear with all macrons in place. However, in most nonspecialized text macrons would not be used with familiar place names: Tokyo, Kyoto, Osaka, Kobe, Honshu, Hokkaido, Kyushu.

The provincial system was abolished in 1871, but the old names remain as sources of regional pride and identity. Other regional names are also encountered, such as Tōhoku, for northern Honshu; Kantō, for the Tokyo area; Chūbu, for central Japan and Nagoya; Kansai and Kinki, for the Kyoto–Osaka region; Chūgoku, for southwestern Honshu. There are numerous others, reflecting Japan's long feudal history.

In general works it is often helpful to roughly locate a Japanese city or prefecture with a descriptive directional tag, e.g., "Morioka, a city in northern Honshu."

Before Meiji, Tokyo (the name means "Eastern Capital") was known as Edo. "Tokyo" should never be used anachronistically for "Edo" or vice versa.

Aichi	Hyōgo	Miyazaki	Shimane
Akita	Ibaraki	Nagano	Shizuoka
Aomori	Ishikawa	Nagasaki	Tochigi
Chiba	Iwate	Nara	Tokushima
Ehime	Kagawa	Niigata	Tōkyō
Fukui	Kagoshima	Ōita	Tottori
Fukuoka	Kanagawa	Okayama	Toyama
Fukushima	Kōchi	Okinawa	Wakayama
Gifu	Kumamoto	Ōsaka	Yamagata
Gunma	Kyōto	Saga	Yamaguchi
Hiroshima	Mie	Saitama	Yamanashi
Hokkaidō	Miyagi	Shiga	

Provinces

Pre-Meiji (1868) provincial names are encountered frequently in literary and historical works.

Aki	Hitachi	Kii	Settsu
Awa	Hizen	Kōzuke	Shima
Awaji	Hōki	Mikawa	Shimōsa
Bingo	Hyūga	Mimasaka	Shimotsuke
Bitchū	Iga	Mino	Shinano
Bizen	Iki	Musashi	Suō
Bungo	Inaba	Mutsu	Suruga
Buzen	Ise	Nagato	Tajima
Chikugo	Iwami	Noto	Tanba
Chikuzen	Iyo	Oki	Tango
Dewa	Izu	Ōmi	Tosa
Echigo	Izumi	Ōsumi	Tōtōmi
Echizen	Izumo	Owari	Tsushima
Etchū	Kaga	Sado	Wakasa
Harima	Kai	Sagami	Yamashiro
Hida	Kawachi	Sanuki	Yamato
Higo	Kazusa	Satsuma	

Prefectures and Principal Cities

N

0 — 100 — 200 miles
0 — 100 — 200 — 300 km

Sea of Okhotsk

HOKKAIDŌ

Sapporo

Sea of Japan

Nemuro Strait

Tsugaru Strait

Aomori
AOMORI

AKITA
Morioka

Akita
IWATE

YAMA-GATA
MIYAGI

Yama-gata
Sendai

HONSHŪ

Sado

Niigata
Fukushima

NIIGATA
FUKUSHIMA

ISHIKAWA
Toyama
GUNMA
TOCHIGI

Kanazawa
TOYAMA
Nagano
Maebashi
Utsunomiya
Mito

Fukui
SAITAMA
IBARAKI

OKI ISLANDS

GIFU
NAGANO
Urawa
Chiba

FUKUI
Kōfu
TOKYO

TOTTORI
Gifu
YAMA-NASHI
CHIBA

Matsue
Tottori
KYŌTO
SHIGA
Yokohama

SHIMANE
Nagoya
Shizuoka
KANA-GAWA

OKAYAMA
HYŌGO
Kyōto
Ōtsu

HIROSHIMA
Okayama
Kōbe
Osaka
AICHI
SHIZUOKA

YAMAGUCHI
Hiroshima
Taka-matsu
MIE
Ōshima

Yama-guchi
KAGAWA
ŌSAKA
Nara

FUKUOKA
EHIME
Tokushima
NARA

Fukuoka
Matsu-yama
Kōchi
TOKU-SHIMA
WAKAYAMA
Wakayama

SAGA
Saga
Ōita
KŌCHI

NAGA-SAKI
Kuma-moto
ŌITA
SHIKOKU

Nagasaki
KUMA-MOTO
MIYAZAKI

KAGOSHIMA
Miyazaki

Kagoshima
KYŪSHŪ

Tanegashima

Yakushima

Tsushima
Korea Strait

Pacific Ocean

East China Sea

Amami Ōshima

OKINAWA ISLANDS

OKINAWA

Naha

NUMBERS

Problems in handling large Japanese numbers are most frequently encountered in material related to finance and economics, such as company annual reports and government-issued budgetary data. Japanese use the units *man* (10,000), *oku* (100 million), and *chō* (1 trillion) in conversation and in written texts, and it is extremely easy for translators and writers to shift one or two zeroes in the wrong direction when converting large numbers for publication in English. Common sense will often be a clue that something has gone wrong in the calculation (giving a city's population as 32 million instead of 3.2 million for example). But the best rule is: Always double-check large numbers derived from Japanese sources.

FOR CURRENCY, USE A CALCULATOR!

In specialized material you can keep currency amounts in yen. In material for general readers, however, currency amounts should also be converted into dollars (or whatever currency is appropriate for your readership). $US amounts generally involve reducing the yen amount by several decimals, since (in the late 1990s) $1 is equal to somewhere between ¥110 and ¥150. Check all currency conversions carefully, *after* you check large-number conversions. A few currency examples figured at the rate $1 = ¥125 are

¥10,000	$80
¥1 million	$8,000
¥1 *oku*	$800,000
¥1 *chō*	$8 billion

NUMBER	JAPANESE	ENGLISH
0		zero
1	ichi	one
10	jū	ten
100	hyaku	hundred
1,000	sen	thousand
10,000	man	ten thousand
100,000	jū man	hundred thousand
1,000,000	hyaku man	million
10,000,000	sen man	ten million
100,000,000	oku	hundred million
1,000,000,000	jū oku	billion [thousand million*]
10,000,000,000	hyaku oku	ten billion
100,000,000,000	sen oku	hundred billion
1,000,000,000,000	chō	trillion [billion*]
10,000,000,000,000	jū chō	ten trillion
100,000,000,000,000	hyaku chō	hundred trillion
1,000,000,000,000,000	sen chō	quadrillion
10,000,000,000,000,000		ten quadrillion

*British usage

UNITS OF MEASURE

Linear Measure

1	*rin*			=	.012	inch	=	.303 millimeter
10	*rin*	=	1 *bu*	=	.12	inch	=	3.03 millimeters
10	*bu*	=	1 *sun*	=	1.20	inches	=	30.3 millimeters
10	*sun*	=	1 *shaku*	=	.994	foot	=	30.3 centimeters
6	*shaku*	=	1 *ken*	=	1.99	yards	=	1.82 meters
6	*shaku*	=	1 *hiro*	=	.944	fathom	=	1.82 meters
10	*shaku*	=	1 *jō*	=	3.31	yards	=	3.03 meters
60	*ken*	=	1 *chō*	=	119.0	yards	=	109 meters
36	*chō*	=	1 *ri*	=	2.44	miles	=	3.93 kilometers
1	*kairi*			=	1.0	naut. mile	=	1,852 meters

Square Measure

1	sq. *ken*	=	1 *tsubo*	=	3.95	sq. yards	=	3.31 sq. meters
1	sq. *ken*	=	1 *bu*	=	3.95	sq. yards	=	3.31 sq. meters
30	*bu*	=	1 *se*	=	119	sq. yards	=	99.3 sq. meters
10	*se*	=	1 *tan*	=	.245	acre	=	993 sq. meters
10	*tan*	=	1 *chō*	=	2.45	acres	=	.992 hectare

Volume Measure

1	*shaku*			=	.0384	pint	=	.018 liter
10	*shaku*	=	1 *gō*	=	.384	pint	=	.18 liter
10	*gō*	=	1 *shō*	=	1.92	quarts	=	1.8 liters
10	*shō*	=	1 *to*	=	4.77	gallons	=	18 liters
10	*to*	=	1 *koku*	=	47.7	gallons	=	180 liters
				or	5.12	bushels		

Weights

1	*monme*			=	.1325	ounce	=	3.75 grams
100	*monme*	=	1 *hyakume*	=	13.25	ounces	=	375 grams
160	*monme*	=	1 *kin*	=	1.32	pounds	=	.6 kilogram
1,000	*monme*	=	1 *kan*					
		or	1 *kanme*	=	8.72	pounds	=	3.75 kilograms
100	*kin*	=	1 *bikoro*	=	132	pounds	=	60 kilograms

TRADITIONAL UNITS OF MEASURE

The Japanese units of measure on this page have in many fields, such as science and industry, been supplanted by the same metric units used in the West. However, traditional units still appear in premodern writings as well as in the arts and building trades. A *tsubo* is still the most common unit used in discussions of floor dimensions, for example. Frequently heard, less formally, is *jō*, which refers to the area taken up by a single tatami mat. Tatami sizes differ according to region and type of construction, so the measurement is inherently inaccurate.

Note that all English measures in the table here are those used in the United States.

IMPERIAL REIGNS AND HISTORICAL ERAS

Until the beginning of the Meiji era (1868), years were referred to by names and numbers in a system based on the reigns of emperors or empresses. Each time a new ruler took the throne, the name of the era (*nengō*) changed and the years were numbered, starting with 1, throughout that reign or until a new era was declared in recognition of some significant event. Today, Western dates and *nengō* are used in tandem. In the table below are all the imperial reigns and the *nengō* they comprise, listed chronologically, with their Western equivalents. In the table beginning on page 61, the era names are presented in alphabetical order.

NOTE

Early *nengō* are highly suspect; the first fourteen are considered legendary, and dates for the next fourteen are not certain.

Empresses are indicated by (F).

All dates shown, until 1873, are by the lunar calendar, as this is how they are typically given in Japan.

Entries in boldface type indicate imperial names and reign dates. Era names are given below the names of the respective emperors and empresses; before Meiji there was frequently more than one era name associated with a single ruler.

1 ....**Jinmu**	21 ....**Yūryaku**	
2 ....**Suizei**	22 ....**Seinei**	
3 ....**Annei**	23 ....**Kenzō**	*Dates*
4 ....**Itoku**	24 ....**Ninken**	*Uncertain*
5 ....**Kōshō**	25 ....**Buretsu**	
6 ....**Kōan**	26 ....**Keitai**	
7 ....**Kōrei**	27 ....**Ankan**	
8 ....**Kōgen**	28 ....**Senka**	
9 ....**Kaika**	29 ....**Kinmei**	539–71
10 ....**Sujin**	30 ....**Bidatsu**	572–85
11 ....**Suinin**	31 ....**Yōmei**	585–87
	32 ....**Sushun**	587–92
12 ....**Keikō**	33 ....**Suiko (F)**	592–628
13 ....**Seimu**	34 ....**Jomei**	629–41
14 ....**Chūai**	35 ..**Kōgyoku (F)**	642–45
Jingū Kōgō (Regent)	36 ....**Kōtoku**	645–54
	Taika	645–50
15 ....**Ōjin**	Hakuchi	650–54
16 ....**Nintoku**	37 ......**Saimei (F)**	654–61
17 ....**Richū**	38 ....**Tenji**	661–71
18 ....**Hanzei**	39 ....**Kōbun**	671–72
19 ....**Ingyō**	40 ....**Tenmu**	673–86
20 ....**Ankō**	Shuchō	686

Legendary

Dates Uncertain

41	Jitō (F)	**686–97**		Ninna	885–89
42	**Monmu**	**697–707**	59	**Uda**	**887–97**
	Taihō	701–4		Kanpyō	889–98
	Kyōun (Keiun)	704–8	60	**Daigo**	**897–930**
43	**Genmei (F)**	**707–15**		Shōtai	898–901
	Wadō	708–15		Engi	901–23
44	**Genshō (F)**	**715–24**		Enchō	923–31
	Reiki	715–17	61	**Suzaku**	**930–46**
	Yōrō	717–24		Shōhei (Jōhei)	931–38
45	**Shōmu**	**724–49**		Tengyō	938–47
	Jinki	724–29	62	**Murakami**	**946–67**
	Tenpyō	729–49		Tenryaku	947–57
46	**Kōken (F)**	**749–58**		Tentoku	957–61
	Tenpyō-kanpō	749		Ōwa	961–64
	Tenpyō-shōhō	749–57		Kōhō	964–68
	Tenpyō-hōji	757–65	63	**Reizei**	**967–69**
47	**Junnin**	**758–64**		Anna	968–70
48	**Shōtoku (F)**	**764–70**	64	**En'yū**	**969–84**
	Tenpyō-jingo	765–67		Tenroku	970–73
	Jingo-keiun	767–70		Ten'en	973–76
49	**Kōnin**	**770–81**		Jōgen	976–78
	Hōki	770–80		Tengen	978–83
50	**Kanmu**	**781–806**		Eikan	983–85
	Ten'ō	781–82	65	**Kazan**	**984–86**
	Enryaku	782–806		Kanna	985–87
51	**Heizei**	**806–9**	66	**Ichijō**	**986–1011**
	Daidō	806–10		Eien	987–89
52	**Saga**	**809–23**		Eiso	989–90
	Kōnin	810–24		Shōryaku	990–95
53	**Junna**	**823–33**		Chōtoku	995–99
	Tenchō	824–34		Chōhō	999–1004
54	**Ninmyō**	**833–50**		Kankō	1004–12
	Shōwa (Jōwa)	834–48	67	**Sanjō**	**1011–16**
	Kajō (Kashō)	848–51		Chōwa	1012–17
55	**Montoku**	**850–58**	68	**Goichijō**	**1016–36**
	Ninju	851–54		Kannin	1017–21
	Saikō	854–57		Jian	1021–24
	Ten'an	857–59		Manju	1024–28
56	**Seiwa**	**858–76**		Chōgen	1028–37
	Jōgan	859–77	69	**Gosuzaku**	**1036–45**
57	**Yōzei**	**876–84**		Chōryaku	1037–40
	Gangyō (Gankei)	877–85		Chōkyū	1040–44
58	**Kōkō**	**884–87**		Kantoku	1044–46

70	Goreizei	**1045–68**
	Eishō	1046–53
	Tengi	1053–58
	Kōhei	1058–65
	Jiryaku	1065–69
71	**Gosanjō**	**1068–72**
	Enkyū	1069–74
72	**Shirakawa**	**1072–86**
	Jōhō	1074–77
	Shōryaku (Jōryaku)	1077–81
	Eihō (Eiho)	1081–84
	Ōtoku	1084–87
73	**Horikawa**	**1086–1107**
	Kanji	1087–94
	Kahō	1094–96
	Eichō	1096–97
	Jōtoku	1097–99
	Kōwa	1099–1104
	Chōji	1104–6
	Kajō	1106–8
74	**Toba**	**1107–23**
	Tennin	1108–10
	Ten'ei	1110–13
	Eikyū	1113–18
	Gen'ei	1118–20
	Hōan	1120–24
75	**Sutoku**	**1123–41**
	Tenji	1124–26
	Daiji	1126–31
	Tenshō	1131–32
	Chōshō	1132–35
	Hōen	1135–41
76	**Konoe**	**1141–55**
	Eiji	1141–42
	Kōji	1142–44
	Ten'yō	1144–45
	Kyūan	1145–51
	Ninpei	1151–54
	Kyūju	1154–56
77	**Goshirakawa**	**1155–58**
	Hōgen	1156–59
78	**Nijō**	**1158-65**
	Heiji	1159–60

	Eiryaku	1160–61
	Ōhō	1161–63
	Chōkan	1163–65
79	**Rokujō**	**1165–68**
	Eiman	1165–66
	Nin'an	1166–69
80	**Takakura**	**1168–80**
	Kaō	1169–71
	Shōan	1171–75
	Angen	1175–77
	Jishō	1177–81
81	**Antoku**	**1180–85**
	Yōwa	1181–82
	Juei	1182–84
82	**Gotoba**	**1183–98**
	Genryaku	1184–85
	Bunji	1185–90
	Kenkyū	1190–99
83	**Tsuchimikado**	**1198–1210**
	Shōji	1199–1201
	Kennin	1201–4
	Genkyū	1204–6
	Ken'ei	1206–7
	Jōgen	1207–11
84	**Juntoku**	**1210–21**
	Kenryaku	1211–13
	Kenpō	1213–19
	Jōkyū	1219–22
85	**Chūkyō**	**1221**
86	**Gohorikawa**	**1221–32**
	Jōō	1222–24
	Gennin	1224–25
	Karoku	1225–27
	Antei	1227–29
	Kangi	1229–32
87	**Shijō**	**1232–42**
	Jōei	1232–33
	Tenpuku	1233–34
	Bunryaku	1234–35
	Katei	1235–38
	Ryakunin	1238–39
	En'ō	1239–40
	Ninji	1240–43

88 ....Gosaga	**1242–46**	
Kangen	1243–47	
89 ....Gofukakusa	**1246–59**	
Hōji	1247–49	
Kenchō	1249–56	
Kōgen	1256–57	
Shōka	1257–59	
90 ....Kameyama	**1259–74**	
Shōgen	1259–60	
Bun'ō	1260–61	
Kōchō	1261–64	
Bun'ei	1264–75	
91...........Gouda	**1274–87**	
Kenji	1275–78	
Kōan	1278–88	
92..........Fushimi	**1287–98**	
Shōō	1288–93	
Einin	1293–99	
93......Gofushimi	**1298–1301**	
Shōan	1299–1302	
94 ....Gonijō	**1301–8**	
Kengen	1302–3	
Kagen	1303–6	
Tokuji	1306–8	
95 ......Hanazono	**1308–18**	
Enkyō	1308–11	
Ōchō	1311–12	
Shōwa	1312–17	
Bunpō (Bunpo)	1317–19	
96 ....Godaigo	**1318–39**	
Gen'ō	1319–21	
Genkō	1321–24	
Shōchū	1324–26	
Karyaku	1326–29	
Gentoku	1329–31	
Genkō	1331–34	
Kenmu	1334–36	
Engen	1336–40	
97 ..Gomurakami	**1339–68**	
Kōkoku	1340–46	
Shōhei	1346–70	
98 ....Chōkei	**1368–83**	
Kentoku	1370–72	

Bunchū	1372–75
Tenju	1375–81
Kōwa	1381–84
99 Gokameyama	**1383–92**
Genchū	1384–90
Meitoku	1390–94

EMPERORS OF THE NORTHERN COURT	
Kōgon	**1331–33**
Kōmyō	**1336–48**
Sukō	**1348–51**
Gokōgon	**1352–71**
Goen'yū	**1371–82**

100 ..Gokomatsu	**1382–1412**
Ōei	1394–1428
101 ....Shōkō	**1412 –28**
Shōchō	1428–29
102 Gohanazono	**1428–64**
Eikyō	1429–41
Kakitsu	1441–44
Bun'an	1444–49
Hōtoku	1449–52
Kyōtoku	1452–55
Kōshō	1455–57
Chōroku	1457–60
Kanshō	1460–66
103 ....Gotsuchi-mikado	**1464–1500**
Bunshō	1466–67
Ōnin	1467–69
Bunmei	1469–87
Chōkyō	1487–89
Entoku	1489–92
Meiō	1492–1501
104 ......Gokashi-wabara	**1500–1526**
Bunki	1501–4
Eishō	1504–21
Taiei	1521–28
105 ....Gonara	**1526–57**
Kyōroku	1528–32

JAPANESE VS. WESTERN CALENDARS

Before the Western solar calendar came into use on January 1, 1873, the Chinese lunisolar calendar was the basis in Japan for dividing the year into months. The starting point and end of a year in the traditional calendar and its equivalent in the Western calendar do not totally coincide. Make sure that any dates prior to 1873 given in Western style have been converted to the actual Western equivalent. To avoid confusion, it is customary in academic writing to leave traditional dates unconverted, referring to them instead as "first day of the first month," or by number (1711/1/1).

While Western dates—months, days, years—are the basis for the modern calendar in Japan, many official Japanese forms (such as bank forms and government documents) still give and require dates in *nengō*.

Tenmon (Tenbun)	1532–55	
Kōji	1555–58	
106 ....Ōgimachi	**1557–86**	
Eiroku	1558–70	
Genki	1570–73	
Tenshō	1573–92	
107........Goyōzei	**1586–1611**	
Bunroku	1592–96	
Keichō	1596–1615	
108 Gomizuno-o	**1611–29**	
Genna	1615–24	
Kan'ei	1624–44	
109....Meishō (F)	**1629–43**	
110 ....Gokōmyō	**1643–54**	
Shōhō (Shōho)	1644–48	
Keian	1648–52	
Jōō	1652–55	
Meireki	1655–58	
111 ....Gosai	**1654–63**	
Manji	1658–61	
Kanbun	1661–73	
112..........Reigen	**1663–87**	
Enpō	1673–81	
Tenna	1681–84	
Jōkyo	1684–88	
113 Higashiyama	**1687–1709**	
Genroku	1688–1704	
Hōei	1704–11	
114 Nakamikado	**1709–35**	
Shōtoku	1711–16	
Kyōhō	1716–36	
115 Sakuramachi	**1735–47**	
Genbun	1736–41	
Kanpō	1741–44	
Enkyō	1744–48	

116 ..Momozono	**1747–62**	
Kan'en	1748–51	
Hōreki	1751–64	
117 ....Gosakura-		
machi (F)	**1762–70**	
Meiwa	1764–72	
118 ....Gomo-		
mozono	**1770–79**	
An'ei	1772–81	
119 ....Kōkaku	**1779–1817**	
Tenmei	1781–89	
Kansei	1789–1801	
Kyōwa	1801–4	
Bunka	1804–18	
120 ....Ninkō	**1817–46**	
Bunsei	1818–30	
Tenpō	1830–44	
Kōka	1844–48	
121 ....Kōmei	**1846–66**	
Kaei	1848–54	
Ansei	1854–60	
Man'en	1860–61	
Bunkyū	1861–64	
Genji	1864–65	
Keiō	1865–68	
122 ....Meiji	**1867–1912**	
Meiji	1868–1912	
123 ....Taishō	**1912–26**	
Taishō	1912–26	
124 ....Shōwa	**1926–89**	
Shōwa	1926–89	
125 ..The Present		
Emperor	**1989–**	
Heisei	1989–	

HISTORICAL ERAS, ALPHABETICAL LIST

This table gives historical eras (*nengō*) alphabetically for easy reference. In text intended for a general audience, *nengō* should be converted to their Western equivalents. In specialized material, provide the *nengō* in parentheses after the equivalent Western date, for example, "1708 (Hōei 4)." Note that the name of the emperor ruling during each era is not included here; imperial names can be found in the table beginning on page 56. A useful resource for converting specific dates is *Japanese Chronological Tables from 601 to 1872 A.D.* (see the listing in **Further References**).

An'ei	1772–81	Chōkan	1163–65
Angen	1175–77	Chōkyō	1487–89
Anna	968–70	Chōkyū	1040–44
Ansei	1854–60	Chōroku	1457–60
Antei	1227–29	Chōryaku	1037–40
		Chōshō	1132–35
Bun'an	1444–49	Chōtoku	995–99
Bun'ei	1264–75	Chōwa	1012–17
Bunchū	1372–75		
Bunji	1185–90	Daidō	806–10
Bunka	1804–18	Daiji	1126–31
Bunki	1501–4		
Bunkyū	1861–64	Eichō	1096–97
Bunmei	1469–87	Eien	987–89
Bun'ō	1260–61	Eihō (Eiho)	1081–84
Bunpō (Bunpo)	1317–19	Eiji	1141–42
Bunroku	1592–96	Eikan	983–85
Bunryaku	1234–35	Eikyō	1429–41
Bunsei	1818–30	Eikyū	1113–18
Bunshō	1466–67	Eiman	1165–66
		Einin	1293–99
Chōgen	1028–37	Eiroku	1558–70
Chōhō	999–1004	Eiryaku	1160–61
Chōji	1104–6	Eishō	1046–53

Eishō	1504–21
Eiso	989–90
Eitoku	1381–84
Eiwa	1375–79
Enbun	1356–61
Enchō	923–31
Engen	1336–40
Engi	901–23
Enkyō	1308–11
Enkyō	1744–48
Enkyū	1069–74
En'ō	1239–40
Enpō	1673–81
Enryaku	782–806
Entoku	1489–92
Gen'ei	1118–20
Gangyō (Gankei)	877–85
Genbun	1736–41
Genchū	1384–90
Genji	1864–65
Genki	1570–73
Genkō	1321–24
Genkō	1331–34
Genkyū	1204–6
Genna	1615–24
Gennin	1224–25
Gen'ō	1319–21
Genroku	1688–1704
Genryaku	1184–85
Gentoku	1329–31
Hakuchi	650–54
Heiji	1159–60
Heisei	1989–
Hōan	1120–24
Hōei	1704–11
Hōen	1135–41
Hōgen	1156–59
Hōji	1247–49
Hōki	770–80
Hōreki	1751–64

Hōtoku	1449–52
Jian	1021–24
Jingo-keiun	767–70
Jinki	724–29
Jiryaku	1065–69
Jishō	1177–81
Jōei	1232–33
Jōgan	859–77
Jōgen	1207–11
Jōgen	976–78
Jōhei (Shōhei)	931–38
Jōhō	1074–77
Jōkyō	1684–88
Jōkyū	1219–22
Jōō	1222–24
Jōō	1652–55
Jōryaku (Shōryaku)	1077–81
Jōtoku	1097–99
Jōwa (Shōwa)	834–48
Juei	1182–84
Kaei	1848–54
Kagen	1303–6
Kahō	1094–96
Kajō	1106–8
Kajō (Kashō)	848–51
Kakitsu	1441–44
Kanbun	1661–73
Kan'ei	1624–44
Kan'en	1748–51
Kangen	1243–47
Kangi	1229–32
Kanji	1087–94
Kankō	1004–12
Kanna	985–87
Kannin	1017–21
Kanpō	1741–44
Kanpyō	889–98
Kansei	1789–1801
Kanshō	1460–66
Kantoku	1044–46

Kaō	1169–71		Meiji	1868–1912
Karoku	1225–27		Meiō	1492–1501
Karyaku	1326–29		Meireki	1655–58
Katei	1235–38		Meitoku	1390–94
Keian	1648–52		Meiwa	1764–72
Keichō	1596–1615			
Keiō	1865–68		Nin'an	1166–69
Keiun (Kyōun)	704–8		Ninji	1240–43
Kenchō	1249–56		Ninju	851–54
Ken'ei	1206–7		Ninna	885–89
Kengen	1302–3		Ninpei	1151–54
Kenji	1275–78			
Kenkyū	1190–99		Ōchō	1311–12
Kenmu	1334–36		Ōei	1394–1428
Kennin	1201–4		Ōhō	1161–63
Kenpō	1213–19		Ōnin	1467–69
Kenryaku	1211–13		Ōtoku	1084–87
Kentoku	1370–72		Ōwa	961–64
Kōan	1278–88			
Kōchō	1261–64		Reiki	715–17
Kōgen	1256–57		Ryakunin	1238–39
Kōhei	1058–65			
Kōhō	964–68		Saikō	854–57
Kōji	1142–44		Shōan	1171–75
Kōji	1555–58		Shōan	1299–1302
Kōka	1844–48		Shōchō	1428–29
Kōkoku	1340–46		Shōchū	1324–26
Kōnin	810–24		Shōgen	1259–60
Kōshō	1455–57		Shōhei	1346–70
Kōwa	1099–1104		Shōhei (Jōhei)	931–38
Kōwa	1381–84		Shōhō	1644–48
Kyōhō	1716–36		Shōji	1199–1201
Kyōroku	1528–32		Shōka	1257–59
Kyōtoku	1452–55		Shōō	1288–93
Kyōun (Keiun)	704–8		Shōryaku (Jōryaku)	1077–81
Kyōwa	1801–4		Shōryaku	990–95
Kyūan	1145–51		Shōtai	898–901
Kyūju	1154–56		Shōtoku	1711–16
			Shōwa	1312–17
Man'en	1860–61		Shōwa	1926–89
Manji	1658–61		Shōwa (Jōwa)	834–48
Manju	1024–28		Shuchō	686

Taiei	1521–28		Tenpuku	1233–34
Taihō	701–4		Tenpyō	729–49
Taika	645–50		Tenpyō-hōji	757–65
Taishō	1912–26		Tenpyō-jingo	765–67
Ten'an	857–59		Tenpyō-kanpō	749
Tenchō	824–34		Tenpyō-shōhō	749–57
Ten'ei	1110–13		Tenroku	970–73
Ten'en	973–76		Tenryaku	947–57
Tengen	978–83		Tenshō	1131–32
Tengi	1053–58		Tenshō	1573–92
Tengyō	938–47		Tentoku	957–61
Tenji	1124–26		Ten'yō	1144–45
Tenju	1375–81		Tokuji	1306–8
Tenmei	1781–89			
Tenmon (Tenbun)	1532–55		Wadō	708–15
Tenna	1681–84			
Tennin	1108–10		Yōrō	717–24
Ten'ō	781–82		Yōwa	1181–82
Tenpō	1830–44			

MODERN ERA CONVERSION CHART

The table below gives year-by-year conversions for all dates of the modern era. For pre-Meiji (1868) dates see the preceding two sections.

Meiji					
1	1868	30	1897	11	1922
2	1869	31	1898	12	1923
3	1870	32	1899	13	1924
4	1871	33	1900	14	1925
5	1872	34	1901	15	1926
6	1873	35	1902	*to December 24*	
7	1874	36	1903		
8	1875	37	1904	***Shōwa***	
9	1876	38	1905	*from December 25*	
10	1877	39	1906		
11	1878	40	1907		
12	1879	41	1908	1	1926
13	1880	42	1909	2	1927
14	1881	43	1910	3	1928
15	1882	44	1911	4	1929
16	1883	45	1912	5	1930
17	1884	*to July 29*		6	1931
18	1885			7	1932
19	1886	***Taishō***		8	1933
20	1887	*from July 30*		9	1934
21	1888			10	1935
22	1889			11	1936
23	1890	1	1912	12	1937
24	1891	2	1913	13	1938
25	1892	3	1914	14	1939
26	1893	4	1915	15	1940
27	1894	5	1916	16	1941
28	1895	6	1917	17	1942
29	1896	7	1918	18	1943
		8	1919	19	1944
		9	1920	20	1945
		10	1921	21	1946

NOTE

In Meiji 5, on 1872/12/3, the solar calendar was adopted, and that date became the start of Meiji 6 (1873/1/1 by the solar calendar).

				Heisei	
22	1947	45	1970	___ from January 7	
23	1948	46	1971		
24	1949	47	1972		
25	1950	48	1973		
26	1951	49	1974	1	1989
27	1952	50	1975	2	1990
28	1953	51	1976	3	1991
29	1954	52	1977	4	1992
30	1955	53	1978	5	1993
31	1956	54	1979	6	1994
32	1957	55	1980	7	1995
33	1958	56	1981	8	1996
34	1959	57	1982	9	1997
35	1960	58	1983	10	1998
36	1961	59	1984	11	1999
37	1962	60	1985	12	2000
38	1963	61	1986	13	2001
39	1964	62	1987	14	2002
40	1965	63	1988	15	2003
41	1966	64	1989	16	2004
42	1967	*to January 6*			
43	1968				
44	1969				

PRINCIPAL PERIODS OF JAPANESE HISTORY

Political Periods	*Cultural Periods*
PREHISTORIC (GENSHI)	
	Jōmon, ca. 10,000 B.C.–ca. 300 B.C.
	Yayoi, ca. 300 B.C.–A.D. 300
	Kofun (Tumulus), ca. 250–552
ANCIENT (KODAI)	
Yamato, 300–710	
	Asuka, 552–645
	Hakuhō, 645–710
Nara, 710–94	Tenpyō, 710–94
Heian, 794–1185	Kōnin-Jōgan, 794–894
	Fujiwara, 897–1185
MEDIEVAL (CHŪSEI)	
Kamakura, 1185–1333	
Kenmu, 1333–36	
Muromachi (Ashikaga), 1336–1573	Kitayama, 1367–1408
Nanbokuchō or "Northern and Southern	Higashiyama, 1449–73
courts," 1336–92; Muromachi, 1392–1573	
Sengoku ("Warring States"), 1467–1568	
EARLY MODERN (KINSEI)	
Azuchi-Momoyama, 1568–1603	Momoyama, 1568–1600
Edo (Tokugawa), 1603–1867	Genroku, 1688–1704
	Bunka-Bunsei, 1804–29
MODERN (KINDAI)	
Meiji, 1868–1912	
Taishō, 1912–26	
(prewar) Shōwa, 1926–45	
CONTEMPORARY (GENDAI)	
(postwar) Shōwa, 1945–89	
Heisei, 1989–	

HISTORICAL AND CULTURAL PERIODS

A period or *jidai* denotes a major historical division and spans several *nengō*. Depending on one's interpretation of events the beginning and ending dates vary slightly, and there is some overlap in different categorizations of periods, particularly for the medieval period. Historians, nevertheless, generally agree on the broad outlines of these divisions. While the major dividing points are based on political events, those who write about cultural and artistic developments often emphasize particular subdivisions within such politically based spans of time. Cultural periods often derive from a particular center of culture.

In most work published about Japan it is customary to distinguish between "periods" and "eras." Kamakura (1185–1333) is a period, while Bunpō (1317–19) is an era.

FURTHER REFERENCES

NOTE

J indicates that a work is in Japanese; you will need some Japanese reading ability to use the resource effectively.

Names of Japanese authors are presented here in customary Japanese order, family name first, unless they are listed otherwise on the title pages of English-language publications.

Most of the books listed here can be ordered from Japan or through bookstores that carry Japanese-language materials. Ordering addresses for Japanese publishers are provided on pages where the respective publishers' books first appear. Names of publishers are romanized according to both title-page and Japanese usage.

Asahi Shimbunsha
Mr. Hirano
Book Export Dept. 2
Japan Publications Trading
P.O. Box 5030
Tokyo International
Tokyo 100-31
Tel: 03-3292-3753
Fax: 03-3292-3764

Asahi Shimbun Japan Almanac. Tokyo: Asahi Shimbunsha. Published annually.

> Comprehensive data on Japan in English and Japanese.

The Chicago Manual of Style. 14th edition. Chicago and London: University of Chicago Press, 1993.

> Authoritative manual for American book editors for over three-quarters of a century. Answers questions on punctuation, spelling, names, numbers, quotations, abbreviations, notes, bibliographies, indexing, and many other tricky points. Organized in numbered paragraphs. Has some information on handling Japanese and Chinese, including a table of Wade-Giles and Pinyin equivalents.

J *Chiezō /Asahi Encyclopedia of Current Terms.* Tokyo: Asahi Shimbunsha. Published annually. CD-ROM available.

> Contains subject sections on terms and topics in international relations, politics, society, economics, industry, science, technology, culture, lifestyles, sports; includes maps, foreign loanwords, abbreviations (acronyms). Terminology sections with English equivalents are extremely useful for translators.

Concise Dictionary of Modern Japanese History. Compiled by Janet E. Hunter. Berkeley and Tokyo: University of California Press and Kodansha International, 1984. Hardback and paperback editions.

> Concise and well-balanced guide to people, places, events, and ideas of significance in modern Japanese history,

1853–1980, with special emphasis on the period before 1945. 650 entries. Salient facts and summaries of debates on political, economic, and social developments. Capsule biographies and analyses. Short bibliographies supply further sources. English entry headings give equivalents in romanized Japanese and Japanese characters. Has glossary of Japanese words that commonly appear in English texts. Appendices give names and dates of office for cabinet members 1885–1980 and lists of major prewar and postwar political parties up to 1981. Thoroughly cross-referenced and indexed.

J *Concise Nihon chimei jiten* (Concise encyclopedia of Japanese place names). Revised edition. Tokyo: Sanseidō, 1987.

Japanese-Japanese dictionary of Japanese place names with short cultural and historical descriptions for each city, town, township, and village. Has *kana* entries in main section plus stroke-number index. Mostly useful for contemporary material.

J *Concise Nihon jinmei jiten* (Concise dictionary of Japanese names). Revised edition. Tokyo: Sanseidō, 1990.

Mainly modern and contemporary names; includes stroke-order index.

Cultural Dictionary of Japan. Edited by Momoo Yamaguchi and Setsuko Kojima. Tokyo: Japan Times, 1979.

Entries in romanized Japanese, divided by subject groupings (traditional arts, dietary habits, clothing, shelter, martial arts, annual events, history, institutions). Does not include many specialized terms.

Sanseidō
2-22-14 Misaki-chō
Chiyoda-ku, Tokyo 101-0061
Tel: 03-3230-9412
Fax: 03-3230-9569

Japan Times
4-5-4 Shibaura
Minato-ku, Tokyo 108-0014
Tel: 03-3453-2013
Fax: 03-3453-8023

Tokyo Bijitsu
2-7 Kanda Tsukasa-chō
Chiyoda-ku, Tokyo 101-0048
Tel: 03-3292-3231
Fax: 03-3292-3234

University of Tokyo Press
(Tokyo Daigaku Shuppankai)
7-3-1 Hongo
Bunkyō-ku, Tokyo 113-0033
Tel: 03-3811-8814
Fax: 03-3812-6958

Kōdansha
2-12-21 Otowa
Bunkyō-ku, Tokyo 112-0013
Tel: 03-5395-3676
Fax: 03-3943-2459

Keizai Kōhō Center
Japan Institute for
Social and Economic Affairs
1-6-1 Ōtemachi
Chiyoda-ku, Tokyo 100-0004
Tel: 03-3201-1415
Fax: 03-3201-1418

Sophia University
7-1 Kioi-chō
Chiyoda-ku, Tokyo 102-8554
Te: 03-3238-3544
Fax: 03-3238-3835

J *Dictionary of Art Historical Terms.* Tokyo: Tokyo Bijutsu, 1990.

Has *kanji/hiragana* entries and Japanese and English definitions. Expensive but good. Chronology of Japanese art included. For translators working in art history.

J *Eibeihō jiten* (Dictionary of Anglo-American law). Edited by Tanaka Hideo. Tokyo: University of Tokyo Press, 1991.

Authoritative English-Japanese dictionary not just for specialists; can serve in place of a Japanese-English legal dictionary. 23-page appendix has *kanji*-English glossary of over 2,000 commonly translated Japanese legal terms. Cross-referenced. 1,044 pages.

Japan: An Illustrated Encyclopedia. 2 vols. Tokyo: Kōdansha, 1993.

Has 11,000 succinct entries on every area of Japanese culture and society, science, and technology. Richly illustrated in color, with excellent indexed atlas and chronology of Japanese history. Entries show Japanese *kanji* for names and terms. Has much more information about contemporary people, events, and society than its 9-volume parent edition, *Kodansha Encyclopedia of Japan.*

Japan 1998: An International Comparison. Tokyo: Keizai Kōhō Center. Published annually.

Contains statistics on population, agriculture and food, industry and services, foreign trade, etc.

Japanese Chronological Tables from 601 to 1872 A.D. By Paul Y. Tsuchihashi. Tokyo: Monumenta Nipponica, Sophia University Press, 1988.

Gives a calendar by which Western dates (Julian calendar up to October 4, 1582 and Gregorian calendar thereafter) can be readily calculated for any day between February 8, 601, and December 30, 1872.

Japanese-English Translation Handbook. Edited by Murata Kiyoaki. Tokyo: Japan Times, 1990.

Includes general list of terms relating to contemporary news and affairs (entries in *kanji*, Japanese alphabetical order); Japanese and English versions of the postwar Japanese Constitution; outline of Diet, government, and bureaucratic organizations; list of Japanese universities giving English names; list of economic and business organizations; names of leading corporations. No English index.

Kenkyusha's New Japanese-English Dictionary. Edited by Koh Masuda. 4th edition. Tokyo: Kenkyūsha, 1974.

The most comprehensive Japanese-English dictionary, with 2,110 pages and 80,000 entries (160,000 phrases) in *rōmaji* in English alphabetical order. Definitions grouped under numbered subheadings, usually from most basic to most specific and idiomatic. Does not include many new words and is not strong on words for exclusively Japanese things. No information on level of usage. Appendixes include list of important Chinese and Korean personal names; list of important Chinese and Korean place names; important terms in East Asian history; list of Japanese government offices, official posts, and special juridical bodies; chart of American/British and Japanese military titles; and list of Chinese readings for Japanese characters.

Kenkyūsha Shuppan
2-11-3 Fujimi
Chiyoda-ku, Tokyo 102-0071
Tel: 03-3288-7777
Fax: 03-3288-7799

Kodansha Encyclopedia of Japan. 9 vols. Tokyo: Kōdansha, 1983.

Most comprehensive reference work on Japan available to date, with 9,714 entries covering 37 categories of information, mainly subjects in the social sciences and humanities. Reliable source of background information on historical, literary, and other matters related to biography, culture, ideas, etc. Content often limited by the interests of the individual authors, but some bibliographical and cross-references are provided. Somewhat dated. Articles by non-Japanese authors should be used in combination with Japanese sources where possible.

J *McGraw-Hill kagaku gijutsu yōgo daijiten.* Translated Japanese edition of *McGraw-Hill Dictionary of Scientific and Technical Terms, 3rd edition.* Edited by Sybil P. Parker et al. Tokyo: Nikkan Kōgyō Shinbunsha, 1984.

Entries in *katakana* or *kanji*. Has 350-page English index.

The New Nelson Japanese-English Character Dictionary. By Andrew N. Nelson. Completely revised by John H. Haig and the Department of East Asian Languages and Literatures, University of Hawai'i at Manoa. Tokyo: Charles E. Tuttle, 1997.

Includes 7,000 main-entry characters with current definitions and 70,000 character compounds. In addition to full explanation of radicals and use of a character dictionary, it contains useful appendices with historical tables, lists of era names, and geographical names. List of Chinese and Korean place names, given in Pinyin and Wade-Giles romanization systems as well as in Japanese readings, has been updated and is particularly useful.

Nikkan Kōgyō Shinbunsha
1-8-10 Kudanshita-kita
Chiyoda-ku, Tokyo 102-0073
Tel: 03-3261-6214
Fax: 03-3222-7192

Charles E. Tuttle Co.
1-2-6 Suidō
Bunkyō-ku, Tokyo 112-0005
Tel: 03-3811-7106
Fax: 03-3811-6953

J *Nihonshi jiten* (Dictionary of Japanese history). Edited by Takayanagi Mitsutoshi and Takeuchi Rizō. Tokyo: Kadokawa Shoten, 1981.

> Contains list of difficult-to-read character compounds (by stroke order). Has color maps of historical periods and ancient, medieval, feudal domains, World War II, etc. Appendixes include list of emperors, female regents, major family trees; table of Buddhist sects, Shinto sects, new religions; table comparing ancient and modern regions.

J *Trend: Nichi-Bei hyōgen jiten* (Trend: Japan–U.S. dictionary of current terms). Compiled by Iwatsu Keisuke and Matsumoto Michihiro. Tokyo: Shōgakukan, 1984.

> Outlines "Japanese" cultural phenomena including kimono, cuisine, traditional house, flower arrangement, tea ceremony, Chinese characters, and sumo. Body of dictionary has subject groupings of terms in *a-i-u-e-o* order (no *rōmaji*). Includes lists of English names of corporate executive positions, major corporations, and names of universities. Has chart of Japanese government organization, giving English names of each ministry, agency, etc. More comprehensive and up-to-date than lists in *Kenkyusha's New Japanese-English Dictionary*. English index of contents. Handy desktop size.

Kadokawa Shoten
3 Fl., 2-13-3 Fujimi
Chiyoda-ku, Tokyo 102-0071
Tel: 03-3238-8521
Fax: 03-3814-6854

Shōgakukan
2-3-1 Hitotsubashi
Chiyoda-ku, Tokyo 101-0003
Tel: 03-5281-1630
Fax: 03-5281-1640

INTERNET RESOURCES

The Internet provides many resources for editors and writers working on Japan-related subjects. Several useful reference sites are listed here, along with a few sites that offer access to the special macron fonts used for romanizing Japanese. Needless to say, Internet addresses and site contents change frequently; if a site does not appear at the address listed here, you may be able to find it using one of the standard Internet search engines.

SWET
http://www.infopage.net/swet

> Information about the Society of Writers, Editors and Translators, including membership and an events calendar. The Launch Pad page lists sites of special interest to editors, writers, and translators. For information about subscribing to the SWET mailing list, see page 79.

Jim Breen's Japanese Page
http://www.dgs.monash.edu.au/~jwb/japanese.html

> An extraordinarily rich site that features the Edict Project, which includes several J-E/E-J dictionaries and text utilities. Also has numerous links to other Japan-related sites, including reference, software, culture, and language-related sites.

Stanford Guide to Japan-related links
http://fuji.stanford.edu/JGUIDE/index_main.html

> Run by Stanford University's U.S.-Japan Technology Management Center, this site provides many useful links to Japan-related sites and educational programs.

J-LINKS Meta-Index

http://www.islandtel.com/j-links.html

> Includes other meta-indices; U.S.-Japan Listserv links; Jeffrey's E-J, J-E Dictionary (searches in English, *rōmaji*, or Japanese); Japanese-language resource links; etc.

Japan Information Network

http://www.jinjapan.org

> Many links and features including statistics on Japan; official names of Japanese governmental and nongovernmental organizations; regional, prefectural, and city information; and much more. Online articles from *Japan Echo*, a current affairs journal, provide useful real-world examples of stylistic choices made by professional editors of Japan-related material.

Macron Fonts

http://www.reddfish.co.nz/

> The Maori language, like romanized Japanese, uses macrons. This site offers free macron Maori fonts (Windows TrueType) and a font conversion tool (RedFish-Macronizer).

http://www.kennett.co.nz/maorilaw/macron.htm

> A free macron Garamond font (Windows TrueType) from the *Maori Law Review*.

http://winz.co.nz/users/navigator/matapihi.html

> Navigator Software Limited sells commercial macron fonts (Maori language) for Windows and Macintosh. Fonts include keyboard drivers for accessing macron characters while typing.

How to Add Macrons to Existing Fonts
http://www.infopage.net/myspace/computers/macrons/

Offers step-by-step instructions for adding macrons to your fonts using Fontographer, a commercial software product available from Macromedia.

COPYEDITING–L Mailing List

An open mailing list for discussing editorial problems, reference books, style guides, related software and Internet resources, and so on. To subscribe, send an e-mail message to LISTPROC@CORNELL.EDU with the following text in the body of the message: SUBSCRIBE COPYEDITING-L YOUR NAME (leave the subject line blank).

HONYAKU Mailing List

An unmoderated list for discussing terminology and other issues related to E-J, J-E translation hosted by JAT (Japan Association of Translators). To subscribe, send an e-mail message to LISTSERV@PEACH.EASE.LSOFT. COM with the following text in the body of the message: SUBSCRIBE HONYAKU YOUR NAME (leave the subject line blank).

NIHONGO Mailing List

An Internet distribution list devoted to discussions about the Japanese language, computers and Japanese, and Japanese culture as it relates to language. To subscribe, send an e-mail message to LISTSERV@UTKVM1. UTK.EDU with the following text in the body of the message: SUBSCRIBE NIHONGO YOUR NAME (leave the subject line blank).

Index

About SWET

The Society of Writers, Editors and Translators (SWET) is an organization of professionals engaged not only in writing, editing, and translating, but also in teaching, research, rewriting, design and production, copywriting, and other areas related to the written word in Japan. Founded in 1980, its activities are planned and implemented by a loosely formed steering committee based in Tokyo. SWET publishes a newsletter five times a year to record the know-how, experience, and insights of members and others in their professions. An annual membership directory facilitates networking among members. Panel discussions, lectures, workshops on professional skills or related topics, and other activities are held to share expertise and experience and seek higher standards in professional work relating to the use of the written English word in Japan.

SWET Resources

SWET supports the SWET-L mailing list, a free service open to non-SWET members for discussion of topics related to English writing, editing, translating, and publishing in Japan. To subscribe, send an e-mail message to LISTSERV@PEACH.EASE.LSOFT.COM with the message SUBSCRIBE SWET-L YOUR NAME (leave the subject line blank).

SWET is also publisher of *Wordcraft: English Writing, Editing, and Translation in Japan* (1991), an anthology of articles of enduring value originally published in the SWET Newsletter.

Contacting SWET

Mailing Addresses

JAPAN

SWET
1-12-30 Minami-chō
Kokubunji, Tokyo 185-0021
Fax: 0423-20-5278

NORTH AMERICA

SWET, c/o Stone Bridge Press
P.O. Box 8208
Berkeley, CA 94707
Fax: 510-524-8711

E-mail

swet@infopage.net

Web Site

http://www.infopage.net/swet

Acknowledgments

Japan Style Sheet represents the combined and refined know-how and experience of many members of SWET, past and present, culled from years of working in various types of publishing, translation, and editorial work in Japan and overseas. We would particularly like to thank the following persons for their contributions to the original and the revised editions: Steve Comee, Becky Davis, Charles De Wolf, Paul Findon, Gerry Harcourt, Peter Goodman, J. W. Higgins, Jared Lubarsky, Martha McClintock, Gretchen Mittwer, Cindy Mullins, Kate Wildman Nakai, Nina Raj, Lynne E. Riggs, Susan Schmidt, Ruth Stevens, Takechi Manabu, Suzanne Trumbull, Fred Uleman, and Christal Whelan.